HOW TO SAIL WITH DOGS

100 TIPS FOR A PET-FRIENDLY VOYAGE

Through exhaustive research and real-life experiences sailing the world with two beagles, we share 100 tips about how to plan, prepare, and potty train for fun, safe sailing with your four-legged crew members. Learn about traveling with pets by air and by sea, potty training and exercising on board, first aid at sea, establishing routines, and keeping your pet SAFE! We also cover detailed customs requirements for U.S.- and European-based dogs entering into dozens of countries in Europe, Northwest Africa, Atlantic South America, the Caribbean, and North America.

By Michelle Segrest

HOW TO SAIL WITH DOGS
BY MICHELLE SEGREST
©2021 Navigate Content, Inc., Gulf Shores, Alabama, USA. All Rights Reserved.

Amazon Kindle (ISBN 978-1-7331322-0-6)
ePub (ISBN 978-1-7331322-1-3)
Paperback Color (ISBN 979-8-6106714-1-3)
Paperback B/W (ISBN 979-8-5180351-4-0)

Edited by Emily Britt

DISCLAIMER

The information provided within this book is for general informational purposes only. The information was gathered through the combination of research, cited articles and resources, and the author's own experiences sailing the world with two dogs. Contained herein are the experiences and opinions of the author.

There are no representations or warranties, express or implied, about the completeness, accuracy, reliability, suitability, or availability with respect to the information, products, services, or related graphics contained in this book for any purpose.

No part of this book, including written passages, video content, and photographs, may be reproduced or transmitted in any form or by any means, electronic or mechanical, including photocopying, recording, or by any information storage and retrieval system, without written permission from the author.

Copyright ©2021 Navigate Content, Inc., Gulf Shores, Alabama, USA. All Rights Reserved.

TABLE OF CONTENTS

INTRODUCTION — 5
DOGS WANT TO BE WITH THEIR HUMANS

CHAPTER 1 — 9
AIN'T NOTHIN' BUT A HOUND DOG
MEET OUR SAILING SEADOGS

CHAPTER 2 — 13
PET-FRIENDLY BOATS
9 TIPS – A PET-FRIENDLY BOAT — 16

CHAPTER 3 — 17
TRAVEL WITH DOGS BY AIR
Our Flight to Frankfurt, Germany — 18
14 TIPS – TRAVEL WITH DOGS BY AIR — 23

CHAPTER 4 — 25
TRAVEL WITH DOGS BY SEA
5 TIPS – TRAVEL WITH DOGS BY SEA — 26

CHAPTER 5 — 27
FIRST AID FOR DOGS AT SEA
Our First-Aid Kit for Dogs — 28
Do Dogs Get Seasick? — 29
14 TIPS – FIRST AID FOR DOGS AT SEA — 31

CHAPTER 6 — 33
SAFETY AT SEA
Avoiding a Pet-Overboard Situation — 34
Managing a Pet-Overboard Situation — 36
12 TIPS – SAFETY AT SEA — 38

CHAPTER 7 — 39
THE GREAT POTTY EXPERIMENT
8 TIPS – POTTY TRAINING ON BOARD — 43

CHAPTER 8 — 45
HOW TO FEED SAILING DOGS
Which People Foods Are Dangerous for Dogs? — 48
Which People Foods Are OK for Dogs? — 49
5 TIPS – FEEDING SAILING DOGS — 49

CHAPTER 9 — 51
ESTABLISH A ROUTINE
"In Port" Routine — 51
"On the Hard" Routine — 52
"At Anchorage" Routine — 53
"At Sea" Routine — 54

5 TIPS – ESTABLISH A ROUTINE	*55*
CHAPTER 10	**57**
WHEN IT'S NOT DOG FRIENDLY	
5 TIPS – WHEN IT'S NOT DOG FRIENDLY	*59*
CHAPTER 11	**61**
EXTREME TEMPERATURES	
Staying Warm	*61*
7 TIPS – STAYING WARM	*61*
Keeping Cool	*61*
10 TIPS – KEEPING COOL	*63*
CHAPTER 12	**65**
THE DOWNSIDE	
CHAPTER 13	**67**
THE UPSIDE	
CHAPTER 14	**69**
A FEW OF OUR ADVENTURES	
A FINAL WORD	**73**
IS IT WORTH IT?	
APPENDICES	**75**
APPENDIX 1 - TRAVELING WITH DOGS BY AIR	
CRATE PREP	*75*
PAC MEASURING GUIDELINES	*76*
APPENDIX 2 - TRAVELING WITH DOGS BY AIR AND BY SEA	77
CHECKLIST Traveling with Dogs	*77*
General Guidelines & Regulations	*79*
7 TIPS – LONG-DISTANCE CRUISING	*79*
Requirements By Country	*80*
APPENDIX 3 – MUST-HAVE ITEMS FOR SAILING WITH DOGS	95
How to Sail with Dogs Survival Kit – SECURITY	*95*
How to Sail with Dogs Survival Kit – SAFETY AT SEA	*96*
How to Sail with Dogs Survival Kit – POTTY TRAINING	*97*
How to Sail with Dogs Survival Kit – TRAVELING BY AIR	*97*
How to Sail with Dogs Survival Kit – KEEPING COOL	*98*
How to Sail with Dogs Survival Kit – A FEW MORE COOL IDEAS	*99*
APPENDIX 4 – BONUS ARTICLES & RESEARCH	101
ABOUT THE AUTHOR	**103**
REFERENCES	**105**
100 TIPS FOR A PET-FRIENDLY VOYAGE	**109**

INTRODUCTION

DOGS WANT TO BE WITH THEIR HUMANS

When Cap'n Jack and Scout first stepped aboard our 43-foot steel ketch, *Seefalke*, they walked around the small vessel and sniffed every corner. Then, tails wagging, they looked up at us, and it was as if they shrugged their shoulders and said, "I guess we live here now." Then they curled up on the settee in the main saloon and settled in.

After traveling more than 9,000 nautical miles—crossing the Baltic Sea, the North Sea, the English Channel, and the Bay of Biscay, sailing along the Atlantic coasts of Spain and Portugal into Africa, to the Canary Islands and Cape Verde, and then across the Atlantic Ocean to Cabedelo, Brazil and up the coast of South America to French Guiana and then to Suriname with them—I am convinced now, more than ever, that dogs just want to be with their humans. It doesn't really matter where.

The beagles were not yet two years old when we began our worldwide sailing journey in August 2018, but they've been sailing with us since they were four months old. Before we moved aboard *Seefalke*, Cap'n Jack and Scout enjoyed many day sails along the Intracoastal Waterway (ICWW), Mobile Bay, and Bon Secour Bay on my 15-foot, open-hull catboat, *Protagonist*. However, they had never sailed overnight or in heavy offshore conditions. And with only day sails, they had never had to learn how to potty onboard.

We learned many lessons along the way about how to keep them comfortable, how to establish routines for them, how to make it through the customs requirements for

Scout and Cap'n Jack always find a way to cuddle with us at port or at sea. They are never far from our side.

This map shows our route from North Germany to Brazil—more than 5,700 nautical miles. We have since sailed another 1,600 miles to French Guiana.

dozens of countries, how to potty train them onboard, and, most important, how to keep them SAFE. All of these insights are shared in this book.

The initial goal was to sail *Seefalke* from her home port in Stralsund, Germany, to Gulf Shores, Alabama, USA. We considered the option of boarding the pups while we sailed for a couple weeks at a time and then returning to Alabama for short periods while at various ports. But the additional expense and effort of

Michelle loves to read while at sea, when conditions allow, and Scout loves to join her.

flying back and forth would have been financially and logistically impossible. Plus, we would miss our sweet pups. We didn't want to leave them at a boarding facility that often, and we wanted them with us. I'm convinced that we made the right decision to bring them with us wherever we travel, even on a worldwide sailing journey.

We spent countless hours talking with other sailors who have a canine crew and did exhaustive research on what it takes to ensure a safe passage for the four-legged family members. We knew that it wouldn't be easy and that cruising with the beagles could limit our ability to travel to certain countries and to enjoy certain tourist attractions along the way. In my opinion, it was an easy sacrifice to make.

We were not afraid of the additional work or paperwork involved. Once we made the decision to take them with us, their safety was the main focus.

We received a lot of criticism from followers on social media about bringing Cap'n Jack and Scout along on the journey. We were accused of putting them in harm's way unnecessarily. At first, the accusations bothered us, but then we chose to ignore the naysayers and focus on the task at hand—keeping them safe, comfortable, and happy living on board with us and sailing in heavy offshore waters with us.

Every day, we are asked countless questions about sailing with dogs, and it is a pleasure to share our experiences. Please remember that every dog is different, every boat is different, and every human is different. The goal is to share our personal experiences and to curate all the research in one place. Hopefully, some of it will help you.

In this book, you will find detailed information about traveling with dogs by air and by sea. You can read about The Great Potty Experiment—what worked for us and what didn't. We include valuable information about the supplies you may need, including medicine and first-aid supplies that are specifically geared toward potential health issues your dog might experience. You will find entry requirements for dogs for many countries and a run-down of some of our experiences in the countries that we visited with our dogs.

The good, the bad, and the ugly side of sailing with dogs is discussed in great detail. I believe it's mostly good, but the downside is honestly revealed, as well.

Our experiences involve sailing with dogs, but a lot of the information presented could also apply to sailing and boating with other kinds of pets.

I can honestly tell you that sailing with Cap'n Jack and Scout is something I will never regret. I enjoy having them with onboard every single day, and I'm convinced that they enjoy the cruising lifestyle. The rewards greatly outweigh the challenges.

Fair winds and wagging tails!

CHAPTER 1

AIN'T NOTHIN' BUT A HOUND DOG
MEET THE SAILING SEADOGS

I am a big-time animal lover with a special affection for dogs.

In 2016, I lost my most loyal companion, Indiana Jones, a 13-year-old terrier/beagle mix, to liver cancer. It was a devastating loss. He went everywhere with me—to restaurants, on errands, kayaking, and sailing in my 15-foot, wooden, open-hull catboat, *Protagonist*.

He slept in the bed with me and never left my side. Mourning his death was difficult. After a couple months, a dear friend gave me some helpful advice. He said, "The best cure for getting past the death of a dog is PUPPY BREATH!" I agreed that maybe it was time to get a new dog.

Most of my previous dogs had a little beagle in them, and I love the breed. So, the search began to find a beagle puppy. I found a great breeder nearby who happened to have two four-month-old puppies, the last two from a litter. I had always had male dogs, so I went to check out the boy.

Cap'n Jack and Scout have been sailing since they were four months old.

I could tell instantly that he was a champion. He was muscular, athletic, and beautiful. But the tiny little female, the runt of the litter, would not stop crawling on my lap and licking my face. She was half the size of her brother. She shadowed the boy dog, never leaving his side.

They were both adorable, with velvety, floppy ears, huge brown eyes, and expressive faces.

I picked up the male, and the female jumped up and wrapped her front legs around his waist and simply would not let go. I was holding them both as the little one held on for dear life, her legs dangling from his body. It warmed my heart, and I just couldn't separate them. So, I took them both home.

When we arrived at my apartment on Plash Island in Gulf Shores, Alabama, I walked the pups to the front yard marina where *Protagonist* was moored. The boy jumped right into the boat, ready to go for a ride. I immediately knew the perfect name for him— Cap'n Jack Sparrow, in honor of my favorite pirate!

I spent a little more time trying to think of a great name for the girl. I noticed that she was really an adventurer, a scavenger, a hunter. She was so small, but she was feisty and had a big personality. She always stayed close to her big brother, who was clearly her protector. It reminded me of my favorite character from my favorite novel, *To Kill a Mockingbird* (Lee, 1960). Scout was the perfect name for her!

Our beagles are a lot like typical human siblings. They play hard. They fight hard. They love hard. Sometimes they wrestle like little wolves, and I think they are going to tear each other apart. But no matter how much they play and wrestle and tumble, they always find a way to cuddle and snuggle while they sleep. It's so sweet!

Cap'n Jack and Scout both adapted well to the water and to sailing. They love to be **on** the water, but don't particularly love to be **in** the water. That's why I don't worry too much about them jumping overboard. But just in case they do, I have tested their aquatic abilities. Like most dogs, they are natural swimmers.

Their beagle noses are able to sniff out the dolphins that live in Bon Secour Bay. The dolphins really love my small, wooden sailboat, so they come right up next to *Protagonist* to play with Cap'n Jack and Scout. There is a lot of wildlife on Bon Secour Bay—pelicans, herons, seagulls, jellyfish, dolphins, crabs, turtles, and even alligators share the island and the bay with us. Even though they are not aggressive, we keep a safe distance from the gators. The beagles are fascinated by all the incredible nature and wildlife that surround us.

The beagles love it when we "unleash the hounds" and allow them to run and play. In Gulf Shores, we have access to amazing dog parks in our area. Their favorite is the dog park at Gulf State Park on Shelby Lake. They love to play with and chase the other dogs. Cap'n Jack is the alpha male and makes friends quickly. Scout is timid, but she just sticks close to her big brother and jumps into the pack when she feels brave. When I travel for work, they stay at an amazing doggie day care center in our neighborhood called Sea Paws (Sea Paws Dog Resort, n.d.). Paula takes great care of them and they get to run and play in the big yard all day long.

While sailing the world on *Seefalke*, we found many private beaches and parks that were dog friendly. It's so fun to unleash them and let them run and play. Often, though, it's important to keep them on the leash, especially in areas like Morocco, Cape Verde, and Brazil, where there are many stray dogs roaming around. I found a few good places to board them for limited periods of time while in Lisbon, Portugal and João Pessoa, Brazil.

Scout always wants to be at the helm.

Scout and Cap'n Jack can see our home while sailing *Protagonist* on Bon Secour Bay.

Cap'n Jack and Scout enjoy hanging out on the warm solar panels on *Seefalke's* deck.

The beagles picked up the art of sailing quickly. If I tell them forcefully to "sit and stay," they go right into the little cabin in the bow of *Protagonist*, and they stay put.

They understand that the command means it's dangerous for them to be in the cockpit.

The command also works on *Seefalke*. There is a safe spot for them in the main cabin that barricades them from getting tossed around the cabin in heavy offshore conditions. Sometimes, they can sense the danger, and they go to their safe spot without being told.

Aboard *Seefalke*, Cap'n Jack and Scout have a safe spot in the main cabin that barricades them from being tossed around in rough conditions.

If conditions are good, they are right there in the cockpit, transitioning to the high side of the boat whenever there is a need to tack. Scout is a natural sailing dog. She wants to be at the helm or the bow with her ears flapping in the wind. Cap'n Jack is a typical pirate and usually finds a cool, dry place to take a nap and chill out. Scout loves to join me in the cockpit on night watches.

And of course, they both have the amazing beagle howl that is so unique to their breed. Cap'n Jack throws his head back and really lets it go. Sometimes it's so powerful it lifts him right off his feet. I love it, but sometimes I feel sorry for the neighbors. Generally, it's Cap'n Jack who does the howling. I always say that Scout is the **hunter,** and Cap'n Jack is the **horn.**

It's a lot of extra work to bring them along on any sailing journey. We have found ways for them to potty on board, eat on board, play on board, and exercise on board. All the awesome tips are shared in this book. Though it requires extra work to sail with dogs, I believe it's worth it. I cannot imagine taking any voyage without them!

CHAPTER 2

PET-FRIENDLY BOATS

Every boat is different. We have sailed on several boats, from small dinghies to 50-foot modern charter yachts, but we have only sailed with dogs on two boats.

It has become natural for me to instinctively scan boats in every marina for its pet friendliness. For example, while in Lisbon, a few berths down from our spot was a beautiful classic offshore cruising racer—a style of boat derived from the Swedisch Skärgårdskryssar design. It was very long but extremely narrow. The deck was covered with highly polished, precious teak, and she did not have a railing of any kind. I didn't even need to ask the sailors if they had pets on board. The point is that some boats are more pet friendly than others based solely on their design.

Throughout this book, *Protagonist* and *Seefalke* are mentioned. These are the two boats on which I have had the pleasure to sail with Cap'n Jack and Scout. I do not think that these boats are perfect pet owners, but this brief introduction might give you some ideas about various details to examine if you are outfitting your boat for sailing with pets. If you are in the process of looking for a sailboat, or if you are upgrading an existing sailboat for pet-friendly sailing, this insight may be useful.

MY SMALL WOODEN DAY SAILER

Protagonist is a 15-foot, open hull, wooden, gaff-rigged catboat. She has a single sail on the single tabernacle mast and a retrievable centerboard.

This particular catboat was built from wood by my neighbor Bob McKay from a New England workboat design from the 19th century. She is a great day sailer—sturdy, robust, and very safe.

Protagonist is a handmade, wooden boat with a classic open-hull design.

13

Before moving onboard *Seefalke* (and whenever spending time home in Alabama), I sail *Protagonist* on the Intracoastal Waterway (ICWW) and in Bon Secour Bay and Mobile Bay in southern Alabama. It's common to take her out for an afternoon cruise or a short lay into the sunset. And there is not a single trip where I wouldn't Cap'n Jack and Scout.

They got accustomed to sailing from the time they were four-month-old pups.

Sometimes Cap'n Jack will sit at the helm.

Protagonist is a good-natured boat that does not heel too much, so the dogs always seem very comfortable. Mostly Scout stays on the lookout, while Cap'n Jack finds a spot to chill and enjoy the ride.

The trips are usually short—no more than a few hours—so potty problems rarely occur. When they do have an accident, they generally happen in the bilge, where the bilge pump and sea water can easily take care of the mess.

During these trips the dogs wear life vests most of the time, and I make sure to bring enough drinking water for them.

They love to be out on the water sailing with me. In fact, whenever I prepare the boat to set sail, they jump into *Protagonist* and impatiently await departure. They quickly got accustomed to sailing and would often instinctively move to the high side whenever we would heel.

With *Protagonist*'s open hull, the dogs always remain deep inside the walls of the boat, and there were never any concerns that they would fall overboard.

I never sailed in heavy offshore conditions aboard *Protagonist*, so sailing with the dogs was not a cumbersome activity at all. Still, I keep safety in mind at all times, even though I generally only sail *Protagonist* on very light day cruises. I am usually close to home and never venture so far that I can't return safely, even when bad weather surprises me.

A SHIP BUILT FOR BLUE WATER SAILING

Seefalke is a completely different boat. Whereas *Protagonist* is an open day sailer, *Seefalke* is a heavy offshore cruiser. She is a 43-foot, ketch-rigged, steel boat, designed for liveaboards and sailing the challenging waters of the North Sea. This is the boat that we chose for sailing the world with the two four-legged crew members.

When Cap'n Jack and Scout moved aboard on August 2, 2018, it did not take them long to accept *Seefalke* as their new home. They occupied the starboard skipper's bunk/couch as their realm, and the little porch over the cockpit as their lookout spot. It is important to keep both clear for them so that they have their personal little areas and a bit of privacy.

Seefalke is a 43-foot, steel ketch. She was built for challenging blue water voyages.

The companionway from the cockpit to the main cabin is deep and steep, so Cap'n Jack and Scout were trained to jump onto the navigation corner seat first. They adapted to that idea quickly.

Since they both love to chew things, it was necessary to hide cables, cords, and other items so that they couldn't

The beagles like to lounge on Seefalke's stern when we are at port. This is a pet-free zone when we are at sea.

destroy them or hurt themselves. One nice side effect . . . the cabin began to look much tidier as we hide things from our nibbling seadogs. One bad side effect is all the dog hair that requires daily sweeping to remove from the space. We could have stuffed a complete set of cushions by now.

The main potty training takes place on the fake grass mat on the foredeck (**SEE CHAPTER 7**). Cap'n Jack and Scout figured out where to do their business after only a few weeks of training and repetition. Sometimes they would hide in the stern cabin to do their business. To fix that, the stern cabin became a pet-free zone with the doors always closed and bolted.

The only major change that was necessary to make the boat pet friendly was to add the sea fence to the sturdy rail. You can read more about this in the "Safety at Sea" chapter (**SEE CHAPTER 6**).

Now, when *Seefalke* is rolling and heeling, the seadogs won't accidentally slide overboard. And because on the stern deck the sea fence was in the way of a lot of sailing gear, it was also necessary to declare the stern deck pet free, at least while at sea.

The bottom line is that neither of the boats are specifically designed to have pets on board, but with a few adjustments it is very easy to make them fit for a four-legged crew.

9 TIPS FOR A PET-FRIENDLY BOAT
- Be sure to outfit the boat with a sturdy sea railing.
- Add a sea fence net to prevent accidental overboard incidents.
- Clear the deck of lines and other obstacles.
- Make the companionways pet friendly by making them less steep and by removing obstacles.
- Protect anything that can be destroyed by chewing.
- Provide the dogs with some space of their own.
- A self-draining cockpit and deck are helpful for accidents.
- If there are any areas that you can't make pet friendly, block them off and declare them no-pet zones.
- If the design of your boat is not suitable for pet safety and you can't outfit it to be safe, don't sail with your dogs on that boat.

CHAPTER 3

TRAVEL WITH DOGS BY AIR

By far, the toughest part of traveling with Cap'n Jack and Scout has been putting them on an airplane and transporting them from Atlanta, Georgia, USA to Frankfurt, Germany. Traveling with them by sea has been easy by comparison.

The planning for a cross-Atlantic voyage took place over the course of several years—intensely for more than a year prior to departure. The decision was made to take the beagles with us in May 2018. That was about three months before we set sail. It was impossible to imagine not being with them for the six to eight months that we estimated it would take to sail from North Germany to South Alabama. There was a lot of work to do in a short amount of time.

Before preparing for what would be required to have them onboard *Seefalke* at sea, there had to be a detailed plan outlining how to cross the Atlantic with them by air. I originally thought I could just call an airline and book a couple of puppy tickets. Easy, right? People do it all the time. That bubble was burst very quickly.

Airlines don't do this anymore—at least not from the U.S. to Europe. Trust me. I called *all* of them. I learned quickly that for a dog to travel overseas on any airline, you must employ the services of an IPATA-approved pet carrier service. IPATA stands for the INTERNATIONAL PET AND TRANSPORTATION ASSOCIATION (IPATA, n.d.). Working with them is now a requirement for ALL airlines flying internationally from the U.S.

There are many capable carriers. I was thorough and interviewed five of them. The prices were similar so I decided to go with a carrier that was local to Atlanta, Georgia, which is where we would make our departure. I found a fantastic one—PET AIR CARRIER (Pet Air Carrier, n.d.), of Alpharetta, Georgia.

I found a direct flight from Atlanta to Frankfurt that was nine hours long. The professionals at Pet Air Carrier helped me with every detail. They secured all the appropriate paperwork and even helped to correctly measure the size of the airline-approved pet carriers. You can find a link to the crates I selected by checking out my **HOW TO SAIL WITH DOGS SURVIVAL KIT** on my website **(SEE APPENDIX 3).**

Pet Air Carrier gave me the logical advice to order the crates early, put them in my apartment, and help the beagles to get comfortable with them many weeks before time for the flight. It's not a good idea to wait until the day of the flight to have the dogs go into the crates for the first time. It can add to their anxiety of the air travel, so it is highly recommended to get them acquainted with the crates weeks before the flight.

The European Pet Passport is a requirement for all dogs traveling within the European Union.

To travel by airline with U.S.-based dogs (and to enter most countries), the dogs **must have** these three things:

1. **USDA-stamped health certificate.** This must be approved by a licensed veterinarian, then shipped to the state's health department for signature and seal. This must happen within 10 days of the flight. For us, I had to ship overnight to Montgomery, Alabama and have it returned before boarding the flight to Frankfurt.
2. **International microchip**
3. **Rabies vaccination** AFTER the microchip has been implanted

Some countries also require:

4. Rabies titer
5. Flea and tick treatment
6. Heartworm treatment
7. De-worming treatment

SEE APPENDIX 2 for a **CHECKLIST for Traveling with Dogs** for all of the research of the requirements for each country that we visited and/or planned to visit during our sailing voyage. You can find more updated information and information about other countries not listed by referencing these helpful websites:

BRINGFIDO (Bring Fido, n.d.), NOON SITE (Noon Site, n.d.), and PET TRAVEL (Pet Travel, n.d.) and by researching the individual country's tourism website. It is very important to do this, especially since many requirements may have changed due to COVID.

We worked closely with our regular veterinarian, Dr. Niesje Langston, in Gulf Shores, Alabama, to secure the proper USDA-stamped health certificate, microchip, rabies vaccination, rabies titer, flea and tick treatment, heartworm treatment, and all the other appropriate pup requirements. She also helped me to create a doggie first-aid kit (**SEE CHAPTER 5**).

The pet crates should be specified to suit the size and weight of each animal.

Cap'n Jack and Scout were secure in their crates after we endured a three-hour customs procedure.

Pet Air Carrier met me at the airport in Atlanta and made sure the pups were checked in and secured correctly. They also arranged to have a pet customs broker help us out when we arrived in Frankfurt to handle all the customs paperwork on that end. I was much more nervous about transporting the seadogs by air than by sea, although the sea details are also long and laborious.

We used LUFTHANSA (Lufthansa, n.d.) as our airline. They have a pet lounge and a lot of experience transporting animals of all kinds. They are famous for making safe and comfortable transports for canine family members. I made an early appointment with a veterinarian in Nidderau to easily get the appropriate European shots and European Pet Passports (EUROPEAN PET PASSPORT (USDA, 2018)) for Cap'n Jack and Scout. The passport became the major document for checking them in and out of most countries, including some countries outside the European Union.

For more information on the "how and why" of European Pet Passports, consider reading this article: **HOW AND WHY TO GET AN EU PET PASSPORT** (Trekkers, 2019).

All the planning and preparation requires hours and hours of work. Some countries have extraordinarily strict entry requirements for pets and require pre-approved import permits. I decided to enlist the help of customs brokers some destinations. I also learned that it is impossible to take a U.S. dog into the United Kingdom on a private vessel, so we were forced to re-route our journey to avoid the U.K. altogether. There are some other countries that prohibit dog entry if the host country is the United States, like Australia and the Dominican Republic. For more detail, **SEE APPENDIX 2.**

FLIGHT TO FRANKFURT, GERMANY

I chose the flight from Atlanta to Frankfurt for a few strategic reasons. First, Atlanta has the largest international airport that is close to my home in Gulf Shores, Alabama. It was necessary to fly the beagles to Germany because that is where *Seefalke* was moored (in Stralsund, which is in the northeastern region of the country). It was important to have a direct flight to avoid the additional anxiety and the extra hassle of a layover.

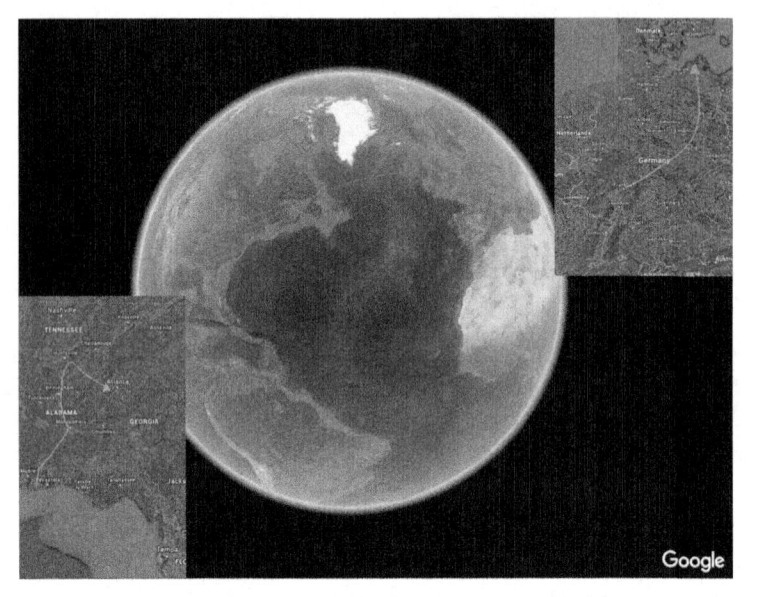

Also, the skipper's mother lives close to Frankfurt (in Nidderau), so it was convenient to make arrangements to stay with her one or two nights before taking the eight-hour train journey to Stralsund. Furthermore, we could make an appointment with the family veterinarian in Nidderau to secure the European Pet Passport.

Getting the seadogs from the USA to Germany required planes, trains, and automobiles.

The beagles and I left Gulf Shores on July 30, 2018 and drove in a rental van (we needed a van to transport the huge airline crates) to my parents' house on Lake Guntersville in northeast Alabama. The next morning, I drove the rest of the way to Hartsfield-Jackson Atlanta International Airport. It was worth all the extra driving to ensure a direct flight to Frankfurt. I did not want to have to deal with a layover.

The dogs and I needed to be at the airport three hours before departure. We met with the great folks at Pet Air Carrier and then went to the cargo area of the airport to check in Cap'n Jack and Scout. All the paperwork was in order, so that was a relatively easy process.

The hard part was leaving the pups in those crates in the warehouse of the airport cargo area while I went to the main terminal to wait for my flight.

We were advised ***not*** to give the dogs a sedative for the flight, and I highly recommend that you avoid doing that, too. Your pet may have other medical issues that could be complicated by taking a sedative.

After nine hours in the air, the skipper met me at the Lufthansa Pet Lounge upon my arrival in Frankfurt. Because of all the customs paperwork required, including a mandatory visit with a veterinarian in Frankfurt, it was another ***six*** hours before we could see the pups and take them far, far away from the airport.

When we finally were able to see them, they looked pitiful. Their cages were covered in pee and poo, and they looked as jet-lagged as me. They couldn't wait to get out of those crates! It was a huge milestone and relief to have the flight to Germany out of the way. I still believe it was more nerve-wracking and difficult to transport them by air than it has ever been to transport them by sea.

We loaded them into a rental car and drove to Nidderau—about a 30-minute drive. The pups were tired and slept for a while before settling in nicely. We stayed the night at the skipper's mom's house and took the dogs to the veterinarian in Nidderau the next day to secure the European Pet Passport.

I took Cap'n Jack and Scout on several long walks and unleashed them to let them run and play in open fields. They loved the exercise and freedom and all the new smells of Germany. We stayed one more night in Nidderau and the next day took the train to Stralsund, Germany (about an eight-hour journey). That is where *Seefalke* was waiting for us.

Cap'n Jack and Scout struggled a little with jet lag and some digestive issues, but they recovered from the air travel quickly. The original plan was to set sail on August 1, 2018, but repairs and upgrades to *Seefalke* delayed our departure until

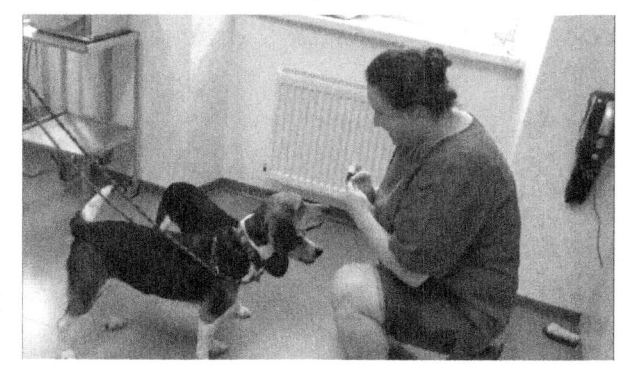

Upon our arrival in Frankfurt, we visited a local veterinarian to secure the European Pet Passports.

August 19, 2018. That actually became a very good thing. It allowed the pups and me to get settled into a routine of living on *Seefalke*. It was important to practice the process of getting the beagles on and off the boat safely, and of course, it was crucial to begin **The Great Potty Experiment (SEE CHAPTER 7).**

I highly advise including a period of time before departure to let your dog adjust to living on a sailboat. Even though the routine changes depending on where you are moored, if you are at anchorage, or when you are at sea, it's important to give them a "settling in" period to make a comfortable adjustment. **(SEE CHAPTER 8.)**

This is what doggie jet lag looks like. We recovered a bit in Nidderau.

After traveling by airplanes and cars, the beagles also experienced traveling cross-country by train.

HOW MUCH DOES IT COST?

NOTE: This is what I paid to transport **two** medium-sized dogs from Atlanta, Georgia, USA to Frankfurt, Germany. Prices may vary for you, but this will give you an idea of what to expect.

Airline-Approved Crates (two)	$170 USD
Pet Air Carrier Services (for two dogs)	
Research/Booking/Documentation/Tracking	$675 USD
Airline Fees	$995 USD
Ground Transportation	$250 USD
Customs Clearance in Frankfurt	$575 USD
Veterinary Services (for two dogs)	
Shots/Paperwork/First-Aid Kit	$1,870 USD
European Pet Passports (two dogs)	$160 USD

HOW TO SAIL WITH DOGS SURVIVAL KIT FOR TRAVELING BY AIR

AIRLINE-APPROVED CRATE

The crates must be IPATA-approved for airline travel, and they *must* be the correct size for your dog. **SEE APPENDIX 1.**

WATER BOWLS WITH HANDLES

Especially for long flights, be sure to buy extra bowls for fresh water for your dog's flight. The small water bowls that come with the crates are not big enough. This is important! Your dog will need good hydration for the flight.

14 TIPS FOR TRAVELING WITH DOGS BY AIR

- ☐ Research and plan early—at least two months before the flight.
- ☐ Locate an IPATA-approved pet carrier if flying from or to the U.S.
- ☐ Order the necessary crates and supplies early.
- ☐ Help your dog adapt to the crate well in advance of the flight.
- ☐ Work closely with your veterinarian to get all shots and necessary paperwork taken care of early.
- ☐ Create and invest in a first-aid kit for your pet.
- ☐ Carefully research the regulations of your departure and arrival countries.
- ☐ Be prepared for long customs procedures at the sites of departure and arrival.
- ☐ Book a direct flight, if possible.
- ☐ Avoid giving your dog a sedative for the flight. Our veterinarian strongly urged us to resist this temptation as it could cause other medical issues for your pet.
- ☐ Visit a local veterinarian at the arrival country to secure a European Pet Passport and other required documents.
- ☐ Have plenty of water and extra food available for the flight.
- ☐ Pack your pet's favorite blanket and toys in the travel crate.
- ☐ Give your dog a chance to run and play unleashed upon arrival.

CHAPTER 4

TRAVEL WITH DOGS BY SEA

Planning and preparation are crucial if you want to sail with your dogs to many different countries. Each country has its own unique set of requirements for dog entry. Some places require periods of quarantine, and some do not allow dog entry at all. In my experience, over-preparing is better than not being prepared at all. The worst possible scenario would be to enter a country and have your dog placed in quarantine. My advice is to do the research before you set sail.

When at sea, Scout and Cap'n Jack can always smell land long before we see it.

If your dog's country of origin is the United States, some countries to avoid are the United Kingdom and Australia. Most European countries have simple requirements for dog entry. Others have extraordinarily strict regulations and require import permits or even the help of a customs broker. It is important to carefully research every possible country that you may visit. Just like when traveling with dogs by air, there are three main requirements for dog entry by boat when entering just about any country:

1. **USDA-stamped health certificate.** This must be approved by a licensed veterinarian, then shipped to the state's health department for signature and seal. This must happen within 10 days of the flight. In our situation, we had to ship the certificate overnight to Montgomery, Alabama, and have it returned to us before we left for our flight to Frankfurt.
2. **International microchip**
3. **Rabies vaccination** AFTER the microchip has been implanted

Some countries also require:

4. Rabies titer
5. Flea and tick treatment
6. Heartworm treatment
7. De-worming treatment

In the appendices, we have included information about all the countries that we researched early in our planning stages. **SEE APPENDIX 2.**

Please remember that the country for origin for my dogs is the United States, but the requirements may be different for dogs with origins from other countries. Also, please remember that these requirements can change at any time, so it is a good idea to use this information as a guide, and always check for updated requirements before you depart, especially since many requirements have changed due to Covid.

Three valuable resources for researching entry requirements are:

BRING FIDO (Bring Fido, n.d.)

TRAVEL PET (Pet Travel, n.d.)

NOON SITE (Noon Site, n.d.)

However, I strongly recommend visiting the main tourist websites of each country for the most recent requirements.

There is much more specific information about how to travel with dogs by sea in the following chapters.

Cap'n Jack has become an experienced sailing dog.

5 TIPS FOR TRAVELING WITH DOGS BY SEA

- Research every country you may want to visit for entry and customs requirements.
- Use online resources like Noon Site, Bring Fido, and Travel Pet for general requirements.
- Visit the website of each country for specific and updated requirements.
- Research countries geographically close to your destination, just in case weather or other factors cause you to change plans.
- Avoid countries that require quarantine.

CHAPTER 5

FIRST AID FOR DOGS AT SEA

What if you are at sea or at anchorage and your dog experiences a bad cut, has an allergic reaction, or falls and breaks a leg? What will you do?

You can't take him to the nearest veterinarian. And even if you are in port, you may not be able to find a veterinarian. If you do find one, you may not speak the language well enough to communicate to the doctor about the problem your dog is experiencing.

You wouldn't set sail without a first-aid kit for the human crew, so don't depart without a comprehensive medical kit for your four-legged crew!

I created a full video about FIRST AID FOR DOGS AT SEA, and keep a full dog pharmacy onboard the vessels that we sail on with Cap'n Jack and Scout. I have used many items in the first-aid kit for dogs along the way. It was expensive to create the kit, which includes many prescription medications, just in case, but it is a worthwhile investment.

I am not a doctor, and I am not a veterinarian. I relied on our personal veterinarian, Dr. Nietjse Langston, for the information in this chapter and in the video. Dr. Langston is not only an excellent doctor of veterinary medicine, but she's also a SAILOR! That means she knows exactly what being on the open water in a sailboat is like for people and for dogs.

She put together a comprehensive first-aid kit for Cap'n Jack and Scout and was gracious enough to let me film the video of her explaining every detail for keeping our canine crew safe at sea! In the video, Dr. Langston discusses the different medications that would be great to have for pets on a boat, and she demonstrates how to apply bandages.

She also gives specific examples of when to use each item in the kit. I believe the video would be helpful for all dog owners, even if you are not traveling on a sailboat. The

OUR FIRST-AID KIT FOR DOGS

- Zofran – For nausea and vomiting. Take it after vomiting starts.
- Carprofen – Anti-inflammatory. Use for soreness of joints or bones, an accidental fall, swollen toe, etc. Use for anything that would require humans to use ibuprofen.
- Tramadol – For severe pain like a broken toe or a broken limb. You can use carprofen and tramadol together for extreme pain.
- Metronidazole – Antibiotic used primarily for diarrhea. Continue for 5 days.
- Diawin – Similar to Kaopectate, but for dogs. For extreme diarrhea, this can be used with Metronidazol.
- Amoxiclav – Use for skin infection, nailbed infection, abscess (use for two days).
- Ciprofloxacin – Use for diarrhea not resolved with Metronidazol; also works for urinary tract infections.
- Acepromazine – Sedative; use for anxiety (dog will get red-eye and be very droopy and drowsy for about 24 hours).
- Prednisone – Anti-inflammatory used for allergic reactions and itchiness. (Benadryl can also work for dogs; check dosage.)
- Interceptor – Heart worm preventive and monthly de-wormer.
- Next Guard – Flea and tick preventive.
- Maxi-Otic – Use for ear infections (treat for 5-7 days).
- Ofloxacin Drops – For scratch on eye or squinting.
- Triple Antibiotic Ointment – For eyes or other skin abrasions.
- Silver Sulfadiazine Cream – For burns or open flesh wounds.
- Vet Wrap (Coban) – Stretch first, roll, then loosely apply without creating tourniquet; it sticks to itself.
- Non-Stick Bandages – Place over wound then put vet wrap on top.
- Silver Nitrate Sticks – For a skin tear with excessive bleeding.

video can be found on YouTube by searching "First Aid for Dogs at Sea" on the Sailors & Seadogs channel. Even though I got this information from an experienced, licensed veterinarian, it is important to consult your dog's vet before using any of these medications. Remember that Dr. Langston has been treating Cap'n Jack and Scout since they were four months old. Every dog is different, and yours may have pre-existing conditions. Having disclosed that, check out the list of items on the previous page that you may want to include in your dog's first-aid kit.

DO DOGS GET SEASICK?

Yes. Cap'n Jack and Scout have not experienced seasickness the same way that humans experience it, but I have definitely noticed that the dogs have been uncomfortable at times. There was only one time that Cap'n Jack actually vomited, and it was a brief episode. Dogs have a very low center of gravity and fantastic balance. That helps them when conditions get rocky. I found this information in the article **HOW CAN WE HELP OUR SEASICK DOG?** (Becker, 2012):

> *"Dogs get motion sickness when the inner ear gets jangled, causing nausea and dizziness. Motion sickness is more common in puppies, and many dogs outgrow it in part because they enjoy being out in the car—or boat, in your case—so much.*
>
> *But the feeling of being sick may worsen over time into fear with similar symptoms, as the animal learns to associate being on the boat (or in a car) with discomfort. If you are boating on a lake or river and your dog is hanging his head over the rail in rough weather only, the occasional solution may be one of the motion-sickness medications people take. Just discuss it with your veterinarian first, because not all over-the-counter medications are safe for pets (some, in fact, are lethal), and you need to know if the drug is right for your dog and what the proper dosage will be.*
>
> *For more severe or frequent cases, your veterinarian can provide a prescription medication that will help your dog. The same is true when anxiety is in the mix.*
>
> *Because your dog only sometimes gets motion sick, however, I would want to know if you are boating on a saltwater body. Thirsty dogs will drink salt water (or take it in while swimming), setting up a cycle where they get thirstier (because of the salt) and drink*

> *more and more. If you're not paying attention, the first time you notice there's a problem may be when your dog throws up.*
>
> *If the problem might be salt water, the solution is to make sure your dog is offered plenty of cool fresh water while you're out on the boat so that he's never tempted to drink the salty stuff."*

DOGS AND MOTION SICKNESS (Flowers, Dogs and Motion Sickness, 2018) is another helpful article. According to this article, dogs don't turn the unflattering shade of green that people do when they're experiencing motion sickness, but there are some signs of dog travel sickness you can learn to identify. These include:

- Inactivity, listlessness, uneasiness
- Yawning
- Whining
- Excessive drooling
- Vomiting
- Smacking or licking lips

The best way to prevent dog travel sickness, according to the article, is to make the atmosphere as comfortable as possible for your dog, keep him in the fresh air, give him plenty of water, and limit his food intake.

For further research, read this fascinating article: **DO ANIMALS GET SEASICK?** (Eveleth, 2012).

FROM MY LOGBOOK: SCOUT'S POPEYE

It was terrifying to awaken one morning to Scout's swollen eye.

Scout's eye cleared within 24 hours of applying the correct treatment.

THURSDAY, AUG. 9, 2018, STRALSUND, GERMANY

I woke up one morning and noticed that Scout's left eye was swollen shut. She was squinting and blinking and seemed to be uncomfortable, perhaps in pain. Fortunately, I had some antibiotic eye drops in the first-aid kit for dogs.

Cap'n Jack and Scout have remained healthy during our sailing journey, and it helps to know we have the supplies we need aboard *Seefalke*.

I texted Dr. Langston, and, fortunately, the time difference between Alabama and Germany worked in our favor. Our veterinarian confirmed that I did the right thing by giving her the eye drops. The swelling cleared up completely the very next day. I think Scout got some dirt or other debris in her eye and that caused the irritation. Dr. Langston told me that blinking is an indication of pain, so I also gave her Carprofen. I was so grateful that there was a complete dog pharmacy on board and I didn't need to go on the hunt for a local veterinarian or rely on the internet to help with the issue.

14 TIPS FOR FIRST AID FOR DOGS AT SEA

- ☐ Consult with your veterinarian before sailing with pets.
- ☐ Secure all required shots and paperwork.
- ☐ Ask your veterinarian to help you create a first-aid kit for your pet.
- ☐ Be aware of any allergies your pet may have.
- ☐ In addition to first-aid supplies, be sure to bring enough of your pet's regular medications or supplies.
- ☐ Your first-aid kit should contain preventive medicines as well as emergency medicine and supplies.
- ☐ Ask your veterinarian if you can text him/her while at sea in case of emergency.
- ☐ Familiarize yourself with the uses for each medication on board.
- ☐ Keep medications in a place that's easy to access when underway.
- ☐ Make sure all medicine is labeled correctly.
- ☐ Research local veterinarians near each port you may visit, just in case of an emergency.
- ☐ Create a "cheat sheet" to help you quickly identify appropriate medications for different scenarios.
- ☐ Learn how to apply bandages, and practice before you set sail.
- ☐ Know the signs of seasickness in animals.

CHAPTER 6

SAFETY AT SEA

Safety is an extremely important topic that warrants in-depth coverage.

If you are reading this book, you are probably contemplating whether to take your pet sailing with you. You may be considering a day trip or an extensive cruise. In addition to all the other considerations, the question about how to keep your pet safe should be prominent in your thoughts. The good news is that the principles for safety at sea with pets and without pets are pretty much the same. However, the bad news is that they are pretty much the same. Let me explain . . .

No one would argue that the safety of human life at sea is paramount. Most pet owners would do almost anything to rescue their pet(s), including putting themselves in danger.

Apart from any ethical questions, that logic requires applying the same or very similar safety principles to pets as to humans.

Scout appears to be smiling while wearing her life vest.

Just imagine the following scenario:

A crew of two humans and one medium-sized dog are out sailing. In rough conditions, the pet goes overboard. The helmsman reacts immediately and steers the boat toward the pet drifting in the water. When the helmsman tries to pull the dog into the boat, the human then slips into the water with the dog. The remaining crew immediately begins the MOB (Man Overboard) procedure. The crew and dog are drifting apart, and after major effort, the crew on board succeeds in recovering the human who went overboard. While all this is happening, however, the dog is lost, and the pet rescue must be abandoned.

This short example is very similar to what happened to the top model Caroline Bittencourt on April 28, 2019 when she was sailing with her husband and her dog, Canjica, off the coast of Brazil. The real-life scenario had a far more tragic outcome, and it shows that a pet in distress translates to humans in distress. In the sad case of Bittencourt, during a gale her dog went overboard, the model jumped overboard to rescue the dog, and her husband jumped overboard to rescue his wife. After one day of intense search-and-rescue efforts, only the husband was found alive. Bittencourt's body was found a day later, washed up on the beach. That is why onboard *Seefalke* we practice safety precautions as much with our human crew as we do with our pet crew.

AVOIDING A PET-OVERBOARD SITUATION

It is important to keep your pet on board the vessel. Even in apparently calm situations, a pet-overboard situation can turn into a man-overboard situation, which can end fatally.

The measures you need to take to keep your pet on board may depend on the size of your pet and their affinity for water. Fortunately, Cap'n Jack and Scout love to be *on* the water but hate to be *in* the water.

That makes them perfect seadogs, because in this case, we only need to take measures against them accidentally going overboard, not jumping into the water intentionally. The following is advice based on our experiences.

Cap'n Jack is safe and secure in his life vest.

INSTALL A SEA FENCE NET

If you are sailing with a pet, it is reasonable to assume that your sailboat is equipped with a flexible or fixed railing. I would never recommend a boat without railing for sailing or boating with pets, especially dogs. Close the openings in the railing using special heavy-duty sea fence. We used cable binders to attach the sea fence to the railing. The

34

sea fence also provides additional safety for humans and equipment. Try to keep technically necessary holes in it as small as possible. Areas where a sea fence would be in the way of sheets or cleats can be obstructed differently.

ESTABLISH AND TRAIN A GOOD-WEATHER POTTY PROCEDURE AND A BAD-WEATHER POTTY PROCEDURE

Seafarers' wisdom states that most bodies found in the water have an open fly. That means they went overboard doing their business over the railing. Pets, apart from well-trained cats, don't usually have the luxury of an indoor toilet.

Onboard *Seefalke*, Cap'n Jack and Scout have been trained to use a fake grass mat that is located on the bow just behind the windlass as the place to potty. It is a great spot, provided the weather is okay and the movement of the boat is limited.

When conditions are calm, we allow Scout and Cap'n Jack to go to the deck without life vests. Generally, they are tethered, and the sea fence provides security. We are also on deck with them in these circumstances.

When the boat is rolling a lot or heeling over, the business becomes a challenge for pets and their humans. It's a risky operation, to say the least. When weather is bad, we have a second fake grass mat that is kept close to the cockpit. When conditions deteriorate, the backup mat is placed in the cockpit for its intended use. It is not the most fun for the two-legged crew, but on most boats the cockpit is self-draining and can be flushed out easily. Practical advice: Clean the area immediately after use so the bad smells won't inspire more sensitive crew members to "feed some fish."

NOTE: When conditions are particularly heavy, I feel more comfortable keeping Cap'n Jack and Scout secure in the main cabin and don't allow them on the main deck or in the cockpit at all. *Seefalke* is equipped with a center cockpit that is four feet deep on all sides, so that is a better option than the deck in most cases. However, in general, if we feel it is not safe, they stay below in the main cabin.

INSTALL LIFELINES AND TETHERING LINES

As an additional safety feature, especially for more water-loving pets than our water-shy seadogs, it is recommended to put out a line from a bow cleat to a cleat closer to the cockpit and attach a tethering line or a leash to it. That way, the pets are able to run up

Conditions this calm are rare. However, we always take precautions when allowing the beagles to be on deck while underway.

and down the deck but can't jump or fall overboard. Make sure they also cannot get tangled in sheets or other moving gear.

We use protective tethers that are reflective and strong enough to support weights up to 90 pounds (Cap'n Jack weighs 35 pounds and Scout weighs 25 pounds). The tethers we use are 25 feet long, which gives the dogs room to roam on the boat, but the tethers can easily be shortened if the dogs' movement and access need to be restricted. They are perfect for keeping them in one spot on the deck or safely secured in the bow.

We experienced severe corrosion issues with tethers commonly available in pet shops or supermarkets. The salt water, especially in warmer waters, will destroy traditional tethers in no time. After that experience, we fabricated our own seaworthy tethers from thin marine lines.

MANAGING A PET-OVERBOARD SITUATION

PET LIFE VESTS

Even if you think your pet is a good swimmer, human sailors aren't the only ones on board who need a proper PFD (personal flotation device). Cap'n Jack and Scout each wear one that attaches securely under the belly and around the neck. I can't stress enough how important it is to have the two handles on top. They allow you to easily grab them in the water—or just hand them into the dinghy, for instance.

MOB ALERT TRANSPONDERS

In the unfortunate event that a pet goes overboard, just like for humans, the first priority is to alert the crew immediately. It cannot be taken for granted that the pet will bark or scream or alert the crew in its own way. For that reason, we use the MOBi overboard indicator by NASA Marine. It is a fail-safe transponder system that consists of a base unit and up to eight active transponders for crewmembers. As soon as the base unit detects a drop in the signal level, it sounds a high-intensity alarm to make everyone on board aware of the situation. The transponders are named, so a quick glance on the base unit shows who has gone overboard. On *Seefalke*, all two- and four-legged crew wear their own personally-identified MOBi transponder.

MOB MANEUVER

The recover maneuver for pets and humans is the same, and we do not want to give a detailed description of the MOB maneuver here. However, there is one major difference between a Man-Overboard maneuver and a Pet-Overboard maneuver. Whereas with humans at least there is a chance that the person who fell overboard can assist in their own recovery, pets most certainly will not be able to. In fact, they may even fight their rescue because they are stressed. Good advice is to keep a retrieval net on board that allows you to catch the pet and pull it back on the vessel. If the pet is heavy, you may want to use the boom or a davit (if available) as a crane to lift the pet on deck.

We have taken **lots** of precautions for the safety of our dogs. Rest assured, our seadogs will always be SAFE at sea! We know you will make every necessary accommodation to keep your animals safe at sea, too!

HELPFUL REFERENCE

BOATING WITH DOGS: 9 SAFETY TIPS (Granshaw, 2013)

HOW TO SAIL WITH DOGS SURVIVAL KIT – SAFETY AT SEA

MAN OVERBOARD INDICATOR (MOBI) FOR DOGS

We use a MOBi (Man Overboard Indicator) from NASA Marine. It's a fail-safe transponder system that consists of a base unit and up to eight active transponders for crew.

SEA FENCE NET

We believe strongly in having a proper sea fence and net to protect both the four-legged and the two-legged crew members. These are easy to install and not very expensive. The peace of mind you will have while at sea makes the time and expense completely worth it.

LIFE VESTS

Human sailors aren't the only ones on board who need a proper PFD (personal flotation device). Cap'n Jack and Scout each wear one that attaches securely under the belly and around the neck. We can't stress enough how important it is to have the two handles on top. Before you set sail, find a way to let your dogs practice swimming in their live vests. They will be uncomfortable at first, but it's also important for them to have experience swimming in the vests when there is not a stressful situation.

HARNESS

When at sea, we prefer to keep the dogs in a protective harness rather than just wearing their regular collars, or we put on the harness in addition to their regular collars. Employing a harness in conjunction with a strong tether is a safe way to keep your pets on board if a huge wave hits unexpectedly or serious conditions cause excessive heeling. The harness wraps around the dog's body rather than the neck, preventing choking or strangling if your dog slips overboard.

TETHER

Tethers limit the movement of the dogs and keep them from roaming too far into harm's way. Restricting their motion is a reasonable safety precaution and can keep dogs safe onboard. **NOTE:** When conditions are particularly heavy, we feel more comfortable keeping Cap'n Jack and Scout secure in the main cabin and don't allow them on the main deck or in the cockpit at all. We have a center cockpit that is four feet deep on all sides, so this is a better option than the deck in most cases. However, in general, if we feel it's not safe, we keep them below in the main cabin.

FOR THE SPECIFIC BRANDS OF PRODUCTS WE USE, PLEASE SEE THE SURVIVAL KIT AT WWW.NAVIGATECONTENT.COM

12 TIPS FOR SAFETY AT SEA

- Apply similar safety procedures for your four-legged crew as you do for your two-legged crew.
- Take all precautions to avoid man- or pet-overboard situations.
- Install a sea fence net.
- Establish good-weather and bad-weather potty routines.
- Have backup plans for bad or unsafe weather.
- If you are unsure that conditions are safe for your pets, keep them in a secure cabin below deck.
- Install lifelines and tethering lines.
- Use light-reflective gear.
- Equip your pet with secure life vests.
- Keep retrieval nets and hooks nearby to help retrieve pets if they go overboard.
- Equip your pet with Man Overboard Transponders (such as MOBi from NASA Marine).
- Establish and practice Man Overboard procedures.

CHAPTER 7

THE GREAT POTTY EXPERIMENT

Without a doubt, the question about sailing with dogs that I am asked the most often is, "Where do the dogs do their business on board?"

It's a great question, and now after a lot of experience and practice, I have a simple answer. There is a fake-grass mat on the bow of *Seefalke*, and that has been established as Cap'n Jack and Scout's "place to go." When at sea and conditions are not safe for the beagles to go to the bow to potty, there is a spare fake-grass mat that is placed in the cockpit. In those circumstances, the humans simply deal with the smell and clean it later when conditions allow.

Simple, right? Well, it took a while to get there. Just like when potty training a dog in your house, potty training on board requires consistency, a reward system, and routine. It's most definitely doable, but it also requires patience.

Here are some excerpts from my logbook that detail some of our efforts during what we call "The Great Potty Experiment."

At first, the seadogs were only interested in playing or sleeping on the potty mat.

Scout and Cap'n Jack were completely uninterested in using the potty mat at first.

AUGUST 9, 2018

Today we started The Great Potty Experiment. The time had come to begin the onboard potty training for the seadogs. We set out a mat that looks and feels like grass, but the pups were not convinced.

Granted, we made a huge mistake by laying the mat out on the pier and letting them nap on it for a while. A friend on Instagram suggested we place a "scent" on it–that is, a sample of their own pee or poo, so they would know what to do.

So, I took the dogs for a walk and got a sample. I placed the mat onboard the boat and strategically placed the sample on the mat. Cap'n Jack immediately sniffed the sample, then peed on the mat.

I thought to myself, this is going to be EASY! But, stay tuned . . .

AUGUST 10, 2018

Day 2 of The Great Potty Experiment was a total bust! While the skipper was running errands to collect provisions, I worked on the training. I put the pups on their leashes and walked them bow to stern to bow to stern about a million times, stopping at the potty mat each time and commanding them to "potty." After 2.5 hours of this, I finally gave up and took them for a walk. They both did their business about 20 feet from the boat. The seadogs definitely won that battle!

AUGUST 11, 2018

The skipper decided to start a massive DIY project. Since the seadogs were virtually uninterested in the patch of fake grass, he went to the home improvement store and purchased some wood, dirt, grass seedlings, and fertilizer. He is convinced that the dogs need REAL GRASS on board for the potty training. He is building a little dog yard. I am skeptical, but I'm willing to try anything!

AUGUST 14, 2018

The skipper continued to work on his potty yard project. The seedlings were not growing, so we decided to "borrow" some grass and do a little transplant.

Not much progress on that end, but we are hoping this will work. The good news is the pups don't want to potty

The dog yard was a huge hit in the Stralsund marina. If only the seadogs had been half as interested as those passing by *Seefalke*.

We tried moving the potty mat to different spots on the boat, but Cap'n Jack and Scout remained uninterested in using it for its intended purpose.

on the boat. The bad news is the pups don't want to potty on the boat.

One thing is certain: our little "garden" is getting a lot of attention in the marina. People walk by and ask us if we are growing vegetables or herbs. Then they see the dogs, then they immediately understand. Fingers are still crossed on this one, but I remain skeptical!

AUGUST 18, 2018

The dogs are still not that interested in the dog yard. They like to sit in it, but they are not yet using it as a toilet. I think that because we are still in port and they are getting regular walks, they probably know there are options. The real key will be when we get to sea and there's nowhere else for them to "go."

AUGUST 20, 2018

After two days at sea, the dogs are basically "holding it" when it comes to doing their business. They have been uninterested and unimpressed with the dog yard. But now the options are even more limited. While sailing through the Baltic, we faced a gale with 40-plus-knot winds. Unfortunately, the wooden dog yard was destroyed and received a proper burial at sea.

THE GREAT POTTY EXPERIMENT CONTINUES . . .

We switched back to the fake grass potty mat. As we traveled through The Baltic, we were making only day sails, so the pups continued to just "hold it" until we made it to port. We later talked to another sailor with a dog onboard (Molly Gillespie of *Terrapin*), who told us that she learned from her veterinarian that dogs won't hold it longer than it is healthy for them to do so. Eventually, they will go—either on their designated spot or somewhere else.

Once we began making longer passages–for example, a three-day nonstop voyage across The North Sea–the pups began to realize that we were not stopping, and they had no options to go on land.

Cap'n Jack was the first to catch on and use the mat on the bow. We rewarded him with treats and lots of praise. Scout had a few accidents in the cabin before she caught on. She also wanted the treats and praise, and eventually made the connection.

We slowly began to establish an "at sea" routine and an "in port" routine, which will be discussed in the next chapter.

Bottom line: it became apparent that when the pups knew they had options, they would take advantage of that. For example, if they know we are on land and can take walks, they do their business on the walks.

When they realize we are at sea and not stopping for a while, though, they use the potty mat on the bow. Dogs are territorial and will eventually establish a "place to go."

It wasn't easy. Developing a system, we have learned, takes a combination of effort, patience, routine, and plenty of reward.

HOW TO SAIL WITH DOGS SURVIVAL KIT – POTTY TRAINING

POTTY MAT

You can try to build a dog yard–but it may get damaged or destroyed in heavy sea conditions. Ours received a proper burial somewhere in The Baltic Sea. We recommend a soft fake-grass mat that has the look and feel of real grass. Get one as close to the real-grass feel as you can. But regardless of which kind of mat you use, it's important to establish one place on board that your dog knows is his "spot." The secret is repetition and reward! I also recommend having a backup mat, just in case conditions are rough and you need to place one in the cockpit.

DOG TREATS

Cap'n Jack and Scout love just about anything that can be called a treat. Just be sure to have plenty on hand, especially for the long sailing journeys. If you run out, try a small cracker with a little dab of peanut butter!

POO BAGS

It's important to clean up after your pet. It is simply the courteous thing to do, especially when you are a visitor in a new country. Keep plenty of spare bags on board because you will need them there, too! They are also handy to have while at sea. The poo bags are not sold in every country, so be sure to keep a good supply onboard. Throw the poo overboard, but please do not throw the plastic bags overboard.

FOR THE SPECIFIC BRANDS OF PRODUCTS WE USE, PLEASE SEE THE SURVIVAL GUIDE AT WWW.NAVIGATECONTENT.COM.

8 TIPS FOR POTTY TRAINING ON BOARD

- ☐ Establish a safe place on board that will be your pet's "place to go."
- ☐ Purchase a fake grass mat, or build a dog yard with real grass, and leave it in the designated spot.
- ☐ If needed, place a pee or poo sample on the mat so they will recognize the scent.
- ☐ Put your dogs on a leash and "walk" them to their place on the deck, as if you were taking them on a walk.
- ☐ Use treats, praise, and rewards, and do that consistently.
- ☐ Keep a spare mat on board to use in a different spot when conditions are unsafe to go to the regular designated spot.
- ☐ Establish a potty routine (that may be different on land, at sea, and at anchorage).
- ☐ When it doesn't rain for a while, clean the deck around the potty area more often.

CHAPTER 8

HOW TO FEED SAILING DOGS

Feeding Cap'n Jack and Scout is simple. Beagles will eat anything. When I say anything, I mean ANYTHING! They eat trash and bird poo and clam shells—even though we try our best to stop them.

Of course, not everything is safe for dogs to eat. Fortunately, my beagles are fine with just about any brand of dry dog food, so we have been able to purchase dog food at almost every stop in every country to which we have sailed.

Even in Morocco, where dogs are not often domesticated pets, it was not difficult to find dry dog food at one of the bigger food markets.

If your dog has digestive issues or allergies or requires some sort of special dog food, obviously it is important to provision accordingly.

Don't count on being able to find a particular brand of dog food at every stop you make on your sailing route.

Most of the time the beagles ate dry dog food, but sometimes, particularly at sea when conditions are rough and it may be inconvenient or difficult to get to their food supply, Cap'n Jack and Scout will eat what the humans eat.

THE MENU YOU SHOULD NEVER LET YOUR DOG ORDER

It would be our pleasure to serve your pup regular dog food upon request.

APPETIZERS
- BABY FOOD
- CANDY & CHEWING GUM
- CHOCOLATE*
- CORN ON THE COB
- HUMAN VITAMINS
- MACADAMIA NUTS
- MUSHROOMS
- TOBACCO*
- OLD FOOD

FRUIT & SALADS
- APPLE SEEDS
- AVOCADO
- GRAPES & RAISINS*
- ONIONS & CHIVES*
- PERSIMMONS, PEACHES & PLUMS*
- RHUBARB & TOMATO LEAVES

MAINS
- COOKED BONES
- CAT FOOD
- FAT TRIMMINGS
- LIVER
- YEAST
- DAIRY PRODUCTS

DRINKS
- ALCOHOL
- CITRUS OIL EXTRACTS
- COFFEE, TEA & CAFFEINE
- MILK & DAIRY

FISH
- FISH IN GENERAL
- SALMON
- TROUT
- RAW FISH

* Especially bad for dogs. For a complete explanation of why your dog can't eat these foods, visit:
WWW.CANINEJOURNAL.COM/FOODS-NOT-TO-FEED-DOG/

CANINE Journal

Infographic 1. This graphic was created by the Canine Journal and is reprinted with their permission.

However, it's important to know what is okay and what is not okay to feed your dog.

For example, if we make spaghetti with tomato sauce, we will set aside a bowl full of plain pasta (without the sauce and spices) to feed Cap'n Jack and Scout.

Cap'n Jack sees land. The seadogs are usually hungry when we arrive at a new destination.

WHICH PEOPLE FOODS ARE DANGEROUS FOR DOGS?

According to experts and our research, here is a short list of foods and other items that are dangerous for dogs to eat. This is not a complete list, so please do your own careful research.

- Alcohol
- Anything with Caffeine
- Anything with Xylitol
- Apple Seeds
- Avocado
- Baking Powder
- Baking Soda
- Candy
- Cat Food
- Chocolate (Especially Dark Chocolate & Baking Chocolate)
- Cinnamon
- Coffee
- Corn on the Cob
- Fat Trimmings
- Food Sweetened with Artificial Sweeteners
- Garlic
- Grapes & Raisins
- Gum
- Hops
- Ice Cream
- Liver
- Macadamia Nuts
- Milk & Some Other Dairy Products
- Nutmeg
- Onions
- People Medicine
- Peppers
- Persimmons, Peaches & Plums
- Raw Eggs
- Raw Meat & Fish
- Rhubarb & Tomato Leaves
- Salt
- Some Bones
- Sugary Foods & Drinks
- Tea
- Tobacco
- Toothpaste
- Vitamins for Humans
- Yeast Dough

WHICH PEOPLE FOODS ARE OK FOR DOGS?

According to experts and our research, these are a few of the people foods and other items that are safe for dogs to eat. This is not a complete list so, again, do your own thorough research.

- Apple Slices
- Baby Carrots
- Bread
- Broccoli
- Cashews
- Cheese
- Cooked Chicken
- Cooked Eggs
- Cooked Fish
- Cottage Cheese
- Green Beans
- Ham
- Honey
- Oatmeal
- Peanut Butter (without Xylitol or other Artificial Sweeteners)
- Peanuts
- Popcorn (unsalted, unbuttered)
- Pork (avoid fatty bacon)
- Pumpkin
- Salmon
- Shrimp
- Tuna
- Turkey
- Wheat/Grains
- Yogurt

HELPFUL REFERENCES

FOODS YOUR DOG SHOULD NEVER EAT (Flowers, Foods Your Dog Should Never Eat, 2018)

WHAT FOODS ARE TOXIC FOR DOGS? (Schenker, 2018)

11 PEOPLE FOODS THAT ARE GOOD FOR DOGS (Langsdon, 2018)

12 HUMAN FOODS DOGS CAN EAT AND 5 THEY SHOULDN'T (Moss, 2014)

10 FOODS THAT ARE BAD FOR DOGS (Clark)

For QUESTIONS OR EMERGENCIES, PLEASE CONTACT THE US ASPCA Animal Poison Control Center — +1 (888) 426-4435

5 TIPS FOR FEEDING SAILING DOGS

- ☐ Research human foods that are okay for your dogs, and those that are dangerous.
- ☐ If your dog requires special dog food, don't count on it being available in every country you visit. Provision accordingly.
- ☐ Keep your veterinarian's phone number handy.
- ☐ Keep the phone number for poison control handy.
- ☐ Establish "at sea" and "in port" eating routines. **SEE CHAPTER 9**

CHAPTER 9

ESTABLISH A ROUTINE

Establishing a routine for your pet when you live on a boat is crucial. That doesn't only apply to the potty routine. It also applies to how they eat and how they get exercise. It's all right, even appropriate, for the routine to change slightly depending on the situation. We have different routines when we are in port, on the hard, at anchorage, and at sea.

"IN PORT" ROUTINE

While in port (and by this we mean moored in a marina), we give the dogs daily walks on land, and they get plenty of exercise. Because of that, we feed them normally, which means a cup of food each in the morning and a cup of food each in the evening. Cap'n Jack and Scout are mostly fed dry dog food.

They are generally taken for morning, afternoon, and evening walks. If we find a place where they can be unleashed to run and play,

We take Scout and Cap'n Jack with us everywhere with us, including on this sky taxi in Lisbon, Portugal.

we try to take advantage of that opportunity. Since we usually need to do a lot of real work for our clients while in port and also usually have many boat maintenance projects while in port, the dogs sit with us for long periods of time while we work. The good news is that they have each other to play with, so sometimes they wrestle and play together while we do other things. It's great that there are two of them, because they can keep each other entertained when we are busy with other things.

Sometimes we need to travel for work while we are in port. We coordinate our work travel so that one of us is always with the boat and the pups—only one of us travels at a time. We had one occasion while we were in Lisbon, Portugal, when we both needed to travel the same week. We were able to find a great dog hotel in that very dog-friendly area, so we were able to work that out without sacrificing the dogs' quality of life. That is the only week in an entire year in which at least one of us had not been with Cap'n Jack and Scout.

"ON THE HARD" ROUTINE

On rare occasions, we need to take the boat out of the water to perform critical maintenance. During those times, we continued to live on *Seefalke*.

For example, while in Cabedelo, Brazil, we were on the hard for almost two months and had to establish a totally different routine. At that particular location, it was brutally hot—7-degrees southern latitude, which placed us near the Equator. Long walks were a struggle for the beagles in that heat, so we took just a couple short walks in the evening.

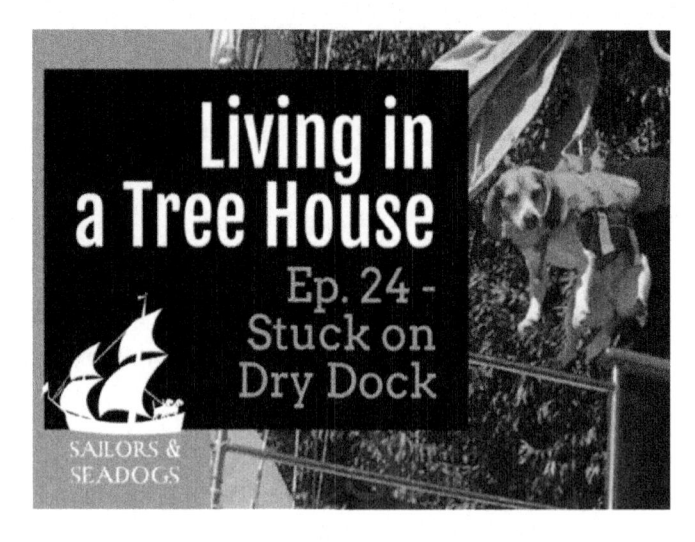

Since they were not getting a lot of exercise, we fed them only in the mornings, with occasional treats for good behavior. We also hosed them down with cold water at times just to ensure they were staying cool.

The biggest challenge with living on dry dock with the dogs was getting them on and off the boat. *Seefalke* sits about three meters off the ground. We have a regular ladder at our stern and a swimming ladder that is attached to the stern. That is fine for the humans to get in and out of the boat, but it would be completely unsafe to carry Cap'n Jack and Scout up and down these wobbly ladders.

We engineered a puppy crane (**SEE CHAPTER 13** to read about our first puppy crane experiment). We strapped on the dogs' life vests, which fasten them in securely. The life jackets have two handles on the top, making it easy to lift the dogs while they are wearing the vests.

We rigged a crane system using two lines attached to a block on the mizzen boom. Attached to the lowering line is a safety strap. The two D-rings of the safety strap attach to the two handles on the life vest. That way we could crane the dogs in and out of the boat with relative ease.

Cap'n Jack and Scout were perfectly safe, although that security requires some effort on the part of the humans. We craned them in and out of the boat twice a day while on the hard—only once in the mornings and once in the evenings.

The routine in Cabedelo was to lower the pups in the morning after they ate breakfast, take them for a short walk, and then take them with us into the marina lobby, which was covered and had decent air flow. The pups stayed with us in the lobby while we worked most days.

We took them on a few short walks and always made sure they had plenty of cold water, then lifted them back onto the boat in the evenings using the puppy crane.

"AT ANCHORAGE" ROUTINE

Depending on the location of the anchorage and the distance to shore, we generally can put the pups in the dinghy and paddle them to shore for exercise and to potty. Sometimes, at anchorage they still potty on their fake-grass mat on the bow, but that is fine. Our main goal is always to avoid accidents in the main cabin where the humans live, sleep, and eat.

At anchorage, we base the pups' food and calorie intake on how much exercise they are getting. If we are going to shore a lot and they can run and play a lot, then we feed them their regular two meals a day. If not, we stick with one meal a day.

We do not let the dogs swim in the ocean from the boat. That is simply our preference as we do not want them to be prey for sharks or jellyfish or other creatures of the sea that could harm them. That is our choice, and you have to make yours. We have seen many other dogs swimming at anchorage or in marinas, and we respect your decision to make that choice.

We saw one dog who was tethered to the boat while swimming, and that seemed like a good idea to keep the dog close and to prevent the current from pushing or pulling him too far away from the boat. Fortunately, our dogs love to be ON the water, but they don't particularly love to be IN the water.

They will wade in the waves that come onshore while they are playing on the beach, but mostly they run from even the smallest shoreline waves. Most dogs are natural swimmers. Cap'n Jack and Scout are good swimmers, but we just made the decision to not encourage them to swim in deeper waters at sea or at anchorage.

"AT SEA" ROUTINE

In the beginning, we struggled a bit when we were at sea—mainly because of the early potty training. But now, we have a comfortable routine for long passages and even spent 20 days at sea without stopping on our Atlantic Crossing from Cape Verde to Brazil.

The skipper is generally on watch from 04:00 until 08:00. The pups wake up when the sun rises, generally around 07:00. They join the skipper in the cockpit and, if conditions are safe, they make their way to the bow for their first business of the day. They are then rewarded with a treat and then they return to the main cabin to play and wrestle. That usually awakens me. The pups and I cuddle a bit and then I feed them a cup of dry dog food each.

Cap'n Jack and Scout sleep a lot on the boat when we are at sea. They also love to just hang out with us in the cockpit or play down below in the main cabin. And they like to sit on the deck. One of their favorite spots is to sit on the solar panels that stay nice and warm. When it's hot, the pups prefer to be on the deck in the breeze or with us in the cockpit. We have tennis balls that they can chase and play with, but they are rarely interested in those. They mostly get exercise by wrestling and playing with each other.

Since we aren't taking them on regular walks, the dogs require fewer calories while at sea. We don't usually give them more than one full meal per day, but they get treats whenever they use the potty mat on the bow. They also may get a little of whatever we eat for dinner, such as a little plain pasta.

When the sun sets and we begin our night shifts, the dogs usually go down to the main cabin and settle in, cuddling with whomever is not on watch. Scout loves to join me in the cockpit for my midnight to 04:00 night watch.

If conditions are rough, Cap'n Jack and Scout stay in the main cabin below. We keep a wooden board in the settee in the main saloon that we can use as a barricade when the boat is heeling. It helps keep the dogs from sliding around the cabin.

It also prohibits them from sliding around when the boat is heeling. If necessary, we tether the dogs down below or in the cockpit to contain them. Their safety is always our main concern. **SEE CHAPTER 6** for more about how we keep Cap'n Jack and Scout **SAFE AT SEA**.

5 TIPS FOR ESTABLISHING A ROUTINE

- Establish routines for your pet based on whether you are at sea, at anchorage, on the hard, or in port.
- Routines should consider how and where they sleep, how and when they exercise, and how much food to feed them.
- Adjust your pet's calorie intake based on how much exercise he/she is receiving.
- Most animals don't have a concept of time, but they tend to understand the order of things. Establish a routine based on order, not time.
- Whatever routines you establish for your pets, always be consistent.

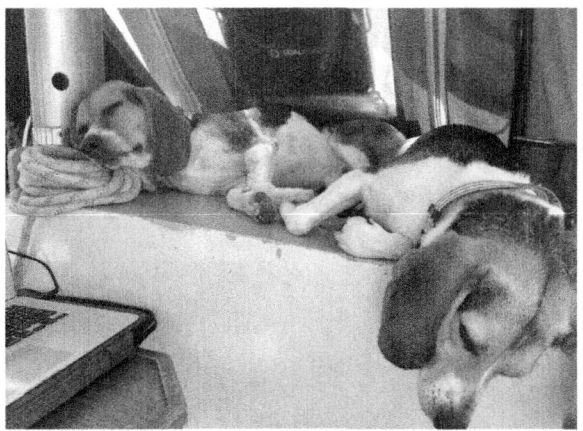

Our beagles have found certain spots on board where they love to lounge.

We all love to visit beaches. Sometimes we can unleash the hounds and sometimes it is not allowed.

When we go sightseeing, the beagles join us. Here we are visiting the Inga Stone in Brazil.

CHAPTER 10

WHEN IT'S NOT DOG FRIENDLY

We did not know what to expect when we made our approach into Rabat, Morocco. Check-in was easy but adapting to local culture required research and an understanding of customary procedures in this Muslim country.

For the most part, we have sailed to dog-friendly countries. Particularly while sailing around Europe, we had no issues whatsoever. Cap'n Jack and Scout joined us everywhere we went.

We could take them with us into restaurants and shops and most tourist attractions. Particularly in areas like France, Spain, and Portugal, it was actually uncommon to see anyone walking the streets without a dog!

Generally, we kept the beagles on a leash, but we were able to find many beaches, parks, and open fields where we could unleash the hounds and let them run and play freely.

However, there have been a few places we have visited that were not dog friendly. Morocco was our first stop where we encountered a different atmosphere for dogs.

The customs process in Morocco was easy. The officials were perfectly happy with us using the European Pet Passports as our main documents. Even though we were no longer in the European Union, the officials considered that a proper document.

In the marina, all was good. We kept Cap'n Jack and Scout secured on their leashes at all times and could walk freely around the marina.

But as we ventured deeper into the city center of Rabat, we experienced a very different attitude. We received puzzled glances and noticed that most people were afraid of the adorable little beagles.

It's difficult to imagine how anyone could be afraid of Cap'n Jack and Scout. But in Morocco, not many dogs are kept as pets. We saw some wild dogs roaming the streets, and we saw dozens of stray cats. But we didn't see one single dog walking on a leash with a human.

We learned that Moroccans consider dogs to be wild animals—not domestic pets. I

As long as Cap'n Jack and Scout have their home base, they have been able to adapt easily to most of the world's cultures—even the ones that are not dog friendly.

suppose it was strange for them to see us taking a couple of wild animals for a walk.

We can understand when we put things into perspective. I compare it to how Alabamians feel about armadillos. We see them everywhere, all the time. We consider them wild animals and probably would not keep one as a pet. It would definitely be odd to see someone walking through the streets of Gulf Shores with an armadillo on a leash.

That must be how the Moroccans feel when they see us walking our beagles. When we posted our **VIDEOS ABOUT MOROCCO**, we received an insightful comment from a Moroccan who explained the local attitude toward dogs. He told us,

> *"To answer your question concerning the whys behind Moroccans not having dogs as pets, not all Moroccans can't or won't have dogs as pets but most prefer not to, the reason being that our religion (Islam) says that dogs have very-difficult-to-wash saliva that don't go away with your typical one soap-filled sponge scrub. In fact, our prophet Mohamed says that if a dog licks a plate it should be washed six times with water and the seventh should be done with soil."*

We appreciate that insight. Part of the reason we love to sail the world is to experience and appreciate other cultures.

We experienced other countries in which domesticated dogs were not as common. For example, in Cape Verde, Africa and Cabedelo, Brazil, there are many stray dogs roaming the streets, so it was always necessary to keep Cap'n Jack and Scout on leashes and not allow them to run and play freely.

Cap'n Jack loves to play on the beach, even when a leash is required.

In Cape Verde, there were hundreds of stray dogs everywhere. They clearly did not belong to any one individual; instead, they were "community pets." They were well-fed and seemed healthy.

They clearly lived on the streets, but because the climate is so mild, it was perfectly fine for them to live outdoors. Some of these dogs would upset Cap'n Jack and Scout, and others would come right up to them and sniff and calmly get to know each other.

It appeared that none of the males were neutered, so of course, it's good that Cap'n Jack and Scout are both "fixed." While the dogs were wild and undomesticated, they did not appear to be a threat to us.

5 TIPS FOR WHEN IT'S NOT DOG FRIENDLY

- Study the culture before visiting a new country to learn about its prevalent attitude toward pets.
- Be respectful of the culture.
- Be sure your dogs are spayed or neutered just in case they run into stray animals that probably haven't been altered.
- If you are unsure of an area's attitude toward animals, keep your dog on a leash at all times.
- In addition to the required shots, be sure your dog is up to date on other shots that could be helpful in foreign lands where other diseases and parasites may be present.

CHAPTER 11

EXTREME TEMPERATURES

Sometimes the temperatures while sailing can hit extremes—for the humans and for the dogs. If you are cold, chances are your dog is at least chilly, although he is covered in fur, which provides natural insulation. If you are hot, chances are your dog is broiling. Dogs don't sweat much; therefore, extreme heat is even more dangerous for your fur-covered crew member than it is for you. Here are some tips on how to battle the frigid cold and the unbearable heat.

STAYING WARM

Even though they are covered in fur, dogs can get cold. Smaller breeds and puppies have a more difficult time battling the cold temperatures. We have seen Cap'n Jack and Scout shiver some while sailing in colder temperatures, but we haven't noticed anything dangerous, so far.

7 TIPS FOR STAYING WARM

- Keep your dogs out of the cold wind and preferably keep them in the cabin where there is some insulation.
- Some sailors recommend a doggie sweater or jacket, but we don't believe in putting human clothes on dogs. Instead, we believe that providing some warm sleeping bags for our dogs to "nest" in does the trick. The pups work their way in to a warm, comfortable spot using just the right amount of help from the sleeping bags or blankets.
- Don't let your dogs sleep outside. Keep them inside where there is some protection from harsh wind and weather.
- Keep your dog dry. If he gets splashed by a wave, dry him quickly to prevent extra chill.
- Feed your dog extra calories to fuel his internal thermostat.
- Don't let your dogs go swimming in the cold.
- Cuddle up. My dogs love to cuddle with humans and cuddle with each other. Human body warmth is a great way to keep your dog warm.

KEEPING COOL

Dogs cannot cool themselves by sweating as prolifically as humans can. Dogs may sweat a little through the pads of their feet, but mostly they will pant heavily when they are battling the heat. When a dog is exposed to high temperatures, heat stroke or heat exhaustion can result. Heat stroke is a very serious condition that requires immediate medical attention. Once the signs of heat stroke are detected, there is very little time before serious damage or even death can occur.

According to the article, **HOW TO IDENTIFY HEAT STROKE SYMPTOMS IN A DOG** (Stregowski, How to Identify Heat Stroke Symptoms in Dogs, 2019), these are the signs of heatstroke in dogs:

- Bright red tongue and pale gums
- Thick, sticky saliva
- Rapid panting
- Dizziness
- Bloody nose
- Bloody vomiting
- Bloody diarrhea

Follow these steps to administer pet first aid for heat stroke:

- Decrease temperature to 104 degrees Fahrenheit, or less, by taking dog to an air conditioned or cool space.
- Soak pet in cold water.
- Place ice packs in his groin area or armpits.
- If temperature doesn't drop quickly, take your dog immediately to veterinarian.

For more, please read **HEAT STROKE SYMPTOMS IN PUPPIES** (Shojai, 2019).

HELPFUL REFERENCES

THE MOST SURPRISING WAYS TO KEEP YOUR DOG COOL ON A BOAT (Pamela)

PET TEMPERATURE MONITOR ROUND UP – KEEP PETS SAFE FROM THE HEAT (Burkert, 2019)

HOW TO KEEP YOUR DOGS COOL IN THE HEAT (Stregowski, How to Keep Your Dogs Cool in the Heat, 2019)

HOW TO IDENTIFY HEAT STROKE SYMPTOMS IN A DOG (Stregowski, How to Identify Heat Stroke Symptoms in Dogs, 2019)

HEAT STROKE SYMPTOMS IN PUPPIES (Shojai, 2019)

20 TIPS TO KEEP DOGS WARM IN THE WINTER (Miller, 2017)

10 TIPS FOR KEEPING COOL

- Always have fresh, cool water for your pet to drink.
- Cover your deck with a tarp or sail. Make sure there is shade for your dog.
- If it's safe, let your dog take a swim in the cool ocean. If your dog doesn't like to get in the water (like Cap'n Jack and Scout), then use a bucket or hose to douse them with cool water as often as possible to cool them off.
- If you have a long-haired dog, keep him well-groomed to minimize his natural fur coat.
- If you have a fan and access to electricity, keep the fan blowing to circulate the air in the cabin.
- While sailing, if the conditions are safe, let your dogs come out onto the deck or into the cockpit so they can enjoy the cool breeze.
- Some sailors use cooling dog beds or cooling pads, which you might consider. We haven't tried those, but we know sailors who use them.
- If you have a fridge or freezer onboard, try wetting a towel or bandana and leaving it in the fridge for a while. Then wrap the cool, wet cloth around the dog's neck.
- Avoid long walks in the extreme heat.
- Be aware of the signs of overheating and respond quickly to counteract them.

HOW TO SAIL WITH DOGS SURVIVAL KIT – KEEPING COOL

HIGH-TECH COOLING PADS

We have never used these, but we know other sailors who travel with dogs who love them! Cooling pads keep your pet cool and comfy with pressure-activated gel technology that absorbs body heat and delivers relief for pets from heat or joint pain. Some cooling pads feature a lightweight, portable, and puncture-resistant material that requires no electricity. That means there's no need to freeze or chill it to maintain a cool surface.

EVAPORATIVE COOLING VESTS

This is another item recommended to us by other sailors, although we have never tried it. This dog cooler comes with a three-layer cooling fabric. Soak it in cold water, wring it out, and put the cooling vest on your dog. It works on an evaporative cooling principle. During the phase transition from liquid water to water vapor, three things happen: the temperature drops, the mesh material helps by wicking water, and the middle absorbent cotton layer that's holding water isolates the heat from the dog's skin.

FURMINATOR

This device was also recommended to us by other sailors to help remove dead hair from dogs' coats. For large dogs with long hair, the Furminator removes loose hair. It reaches through the topcoat to remove loose undercoat hair without cutting skin or damaging the topcoat (when used as directed).

WATER BOWLS

Obviously, plenty of fresh water is critical to keep your dog healthy while on land or at sea. There are some large bottles that automatically dispense water, but we don't like those. We often sail in extreme heat, making it important to consistently provide new, fresh, cool water for the dogs. I love the bowls that have handles or the ones that are weighted on the bottom to prevent accidental spills at sea.

WATER BOY

This is another item that we don't use, but we want to include it since we know other sailors who love it. Giving your pet water to drink in a moving vehicle or boat is a dodgy proposition—most bowls are tippy and shallow, and the water winds up on the floorboards or seats more often than in your dog's mouth. This device holds up to three quarts of water in its reservoir and can be placed flat for easy pet access on the go. Other sailors like this, but we don't like the idea of our dogs always drinking from a plastic container.

BUDDY BOWL

Here is another item recommended by other sailors, although we can't personally recommend it. This is another option if you want a water bowl that is not as likely to spill.

CHAPTER 12

THE DOWNSIDE

We highly recommend taking your dogs with you on your sailing voyages.

We can tell by the constant wagging tails that Cap'n Jack and Scout love being on the boat.

However, it's important to be honest and give you an accurate account of how to sail with dogs, so it's a necessity to address some of the less wonderful things about sailing with dogs.

- **You cannot go into some restaurants with dogs.** This is not tragic. Most restaurants that have outdoor seating will allow you to have your dogs with you. But some forbid it. You simply must be prepared to eat somewhere else if this happens. We mostly eat on board, but we have been in situations where we were disappointed to not be able to dine at a particular restaurant because of the dog restrictions.
- **You cannot see some sites.** If you want to go into museums and other attractions, you may have to leave your dog on the boat, or not go at all. In our case, that was no big deal. We would prefer to climb a mountain or take a hike, and most outdoor attractions are dog friendly.
- **You must walk and care for your dogs.** This isn't so much a downside as an extra energy investment. No doubt, having dogs on board requires extra efforts.
- **There is extra paperwork and preparation.** This was a hassle at first, but once all our paperwork was in order before we set sail, we haven't had to worry about it as much. When we change our route plans and visit a new country, then we simply must check out the requirements before we set sail and make sure all the paperwork is in order.
- **There is an extra customs hassle in some places.** The dogs must clear customs just like the people and the boat must clear customs.
- **There is extra cleaning and maintenance.** Dogs can be messy. Sometimes I wonder how Cap'n Jack and Scout still have hair on their bodies. I sweep and remove from the boat mounds of hair every day. Of course, that is something that is required if you have a dog in a house or apartment, too, and is not specific to living on a boat.

- **Extra crew equals extra responsibility.** The captain is responsible for the lives and safety of the humans and the dogs. That requires extra planning and extra effort.
- **You must avoid some destinations.** This is a deal breaker for some people, but not for us. Some countries (U.K., Dominican Republic, Australia, some countries in eastern Asia, and others) simply do not allow dogs from the U.S. to enter on a private vessel. If there are destinations that interest you that do not allow dog entry, you may not want to sail with dogs.
- **It can be inconvenient to have dogs when you're on the hard or sometimes at anchorage with a small dinghy.** Sometimes creative solutions are necessary and extra effort is required. It's doable, but it's not as simple as if you are only transporting humans.
- **Accidents happen.** Sometimes dogs pee in your bed. Sometimes they get seasick. Sometimes they chew up expensive equipment.
- **One of us always stays with the dogs and the boat.** Because we do not want to put Cap'n Jack and Scout on another airplane, at least one of us must stay with them and the boat at all times. That means we cannot travel for work at the same time or travel together inland to check out something interesting unless we can find a dog hotel nearby.
- **There are extra expenses.** Sailing with dogs is not free. Just like people, they require food, medicine, and other supplies.

Scout and Cap'n Jack have adapted well to their life at sea.

CHAPTER 13

THE UPSIDE

If you have read this far into this book, it would be impossible for you to not be convinced that I love to sail with Cap'n Jack and Scout. For me, the long list of downsides does not really matter. Cap'n Jack and Scout my family, and it's impossible to imagine not having them along for the ride. Here are just a few of the upsides:

- **Companionship.** We are never alone, even when one of us is traveling for work. Our cuddly pups are always right there by our side with their tails wagging.
- **No complaints.** Unlike with people crew, the dogs are always happy and positive!
- **Night watches.** Long night watches can be lonely, but if you have a sweet pup cuddled up next you, it can make any night watch more fun.
- **Protection.** Dogs (especially our beagles with their loud howls) can be a terrific built-in alarm system to protect the ship and the crew onboard.
- **How they greet us when we return from a trip.** We always know we are missed. Whether we just went to the grocery store for a couple hours or a week-long business trip, the dogs greet us with enthusiasm.

Cap'n Jack and Scout are comfortable in the cockpit perch.

CHAPTER 14

A FEW OF OUR ADVENTURES

BATTLING THE BALTIC

AUGUST 24, 2018 – EXCERPT FROM MICHELLE'S LOGBOOK ENTRY, "THE BALTIC SEA—SHE'S A MEAN GIRL"

I settled in and let the pups cuddle up next to me. Probably an hour or so later, I awoke to a rocking boat. I could hear the skipper rushing around on the deck above and caught glimpses through the upper hatch windows of him adjusting the sails. The boat began to tilt and a few more of my well-secured items went flying across the cabin.

Then the pups and I both began to slide. I didn't know it at the time, but we were in the middle of a heavy gale with winds at 38 knots! We were on a 36-degree tilt . . . and, by the way, the skipper was having the time of his life!

I was lying flat on my back on the bunk. My right leg was stretched out straight and propped against the board that generally keeps the pups secure in their bed. My left leg was bent and upright, blocking the pups from flying across the cabin with the various items that were still not secured. I couldn't move to secure the pups in their bunk. I could only hold on to keep them safe, as we were practically vertical at that point.

They were barely fazed at all, but I was using every muscle in my body to stabilize myself, and them, in the awkward position. I think that is what yoga is supposed to feel like—holding one unusual, uncomfortable position as long as possible while your muscles flex and spasm.

I called up to the skipper to be sure he didn't need me. He looked down at me and had the biggest grin on his face. I thought to myself, *"What are you smiling about?"* He was loving the challenge of fighting the storm. "Just keep holding on," he said.

Then an alarm sounded.

It was coming from the bilge, and that meant water had gotten in and risen to a level that would trip the alarm. The skipper told me to check it. *What? Are you kidding me? How will I get out of this position without slamming into the other side of the cabin?*

First, I had to secure the pups. I somehow got them settled and surrounded them with three sleeping bags to give them extra padding. They were now in their usual barricaded bed, which stabilizes them in a confined space and keeps them from moving around in the boat. They curled up and went right back to sleep. *Why can't I be that relaxed?*

While the pups were relaxed, I continued to struggle. However, it helped to know that they were safe.

For the rest of the story, and more like this, please read my 3-book memoir, *Living Life Sideways*.

OUR FIRST PUPPY CRANE

AUGUST 29, 2018 – EXERPT FROM THE MICHELLE'S LOGBOOK ENTRY, "HELGOLAND, OBSTACLES, THE NORTH SEA & PUPPY CRANES"

We were moored at a floating pier next to a massive wall. There is a ladder you must climb to get to the top of the pier. That was no problem for humans, but it was a different story for canines.

Image 48. Helgoland marina wall at high tide.

When we first arrived at Helgoland, the tide was high and the top of the ladder was about 10 feet from the floating pier. I climbed to the top of the ladder, and the skipper (who is about six feet tall) simply handed me Cap'n Jack, and then Scout. We were able to walk them and let them play and explore. No problem.

We returned to *Seefalke* and finished our painting project. Then it was time to take the pups out for their evening walk and potty. But this time, the wall looked different. It was now low tide and now the ladder was at least a 25-foot climb. It was simply not manageable to get the pups off the boat the normal way.

We had an idea. The pups' life jackets are very secure and have little handles on the top of them. They are designed so that if the pup falls overboard, you can simply grab the handles and pull them in (or you can grab the handles with a boat hook). When they are secured into these life jackets, they are velcroed and strapped with clamps. There is no way the jacket will come off of them unless you take it off, and sometimes even that is a challenge.

The skipper rigged a long line with a pulley to create a fairly sophisticated puppy crane. He climbed to the top of the ladder.

There was another sailboat rafted next to us in our mooring. The skipper of that boat came over to help us. I was happy that I didn't have to rely on my own knot-tying skills. The skipper expertly tied the knots at the end of our homemade crane onto the handles of Cap'n Jack's life vest. Then the skipper simply lifted Cap'n Jack up to the top of the ladder—safely and securely. Then we repeated with Scout. Before we get beaten up for this from all the animal lovers, we can assure you that this was safe and secure, and we would never do anything to put the dogs in danger.

Image 49. Helgoland marina wall at low tide.

After all crew members were safely on land, the four of us explored the island and climbed to the top of the red rock mountain to see the observatory of the migrating birds and enjoy the unbelievable view. The pups really enjoyed watching the birds. It was gorgeous and fascinating!

Then we found a huge field and unleashed the hounds for a while so they could run and play. I am so happy we decided to bring Cap'n Jack and Scout with us on this journey. We have gotten a lot of criticism from many people on social media who think we are putting them in danger. But they are part of the family, and we can assure you that they are perfectly safe! I love watching them explore all these amazing new places. They get so excited and take in every sight and smell. I am positive that if dogs could talk, they would tell us they are happy to be along for the ride!

We returned to our mooring and thought about putting the pups back on the crane to lower them back down to the floating pier. It was still low tide. We decided this time that I would walk over to a pier about 50 yards away with the pups.

The skipper then got into the dinghy and paddled over to pick them up at the low pier and paddle them safely back to the boat. That was a much better idea, although the pups didn't like being in the dinghy too much. I actually think they preferred the crane lift.

A FINAL WORD

IS IT WORTH IT?

Dogs require attention. They are expensive. They require additional work and preparation.

But for us, having Cap'n Jack and Scout aboard *Seefalke* is fantastic, and bringing them along on the journey is something we will never regret. The rewards outweigh the challenges by a long shot.

When we see land after a long passage, the seadogs rush to the bow with their long, velvety ears flapping in the wind. They immediately begin taking in all the smells of each new land. Their excitement is contagious! When we set sail, they can feel our excitement as they watch us prepare the boat for departure.

We often receive criticism for bringing them with us, but that's okay. Everyone is welcome to their opinion. But if you ask us whether you should bring your dogs sailing with you, our answer is always an emphatic YES!

WATCH THE COMPANION VIDEO ON OUR YOUTUBE CHANNEL SAILORS & SEADOGS

APPENDICES

APPENDIX 1 - TRAVELING WITH DOGS BY AIR

CRATE PREP

Courtesy of Pet Air Carrier 770-645-1837 www.petaircarrier.com pac@petaircarrier.com

Crate Preparation for Travel
Pet Air Carrier 770-645-1837
www.petaircarrier.com; pac@petaircarrier.com

1 - CRATE SIZE & SPECIFICATION – Pets must be able to stand up, turn around comfortably and have at least 3 inches above the top of the head when standing in a natural position & must space to lie in a natural position without curling in the front legs. Crates must be hard case, non-collapsible, solid top & bottom (no opening on top) & without wheels – "slide locking side fasteners" are NOT accepted. Airlines require that the top and bottom of the crate be secured *with all metal nuts and bolts – no plastic nuts*. If your crate has plastic nuts, you must purchase metal nuts and bolts separately and replace the plastic ones. Whenever possible crates should have handles for carrying. If your pet fits properly in length but you need additional head room, we can provide an extender for the XL and giant crates.

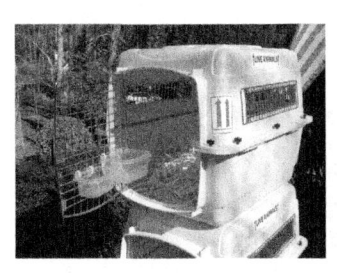

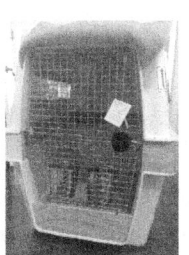

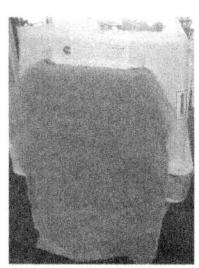

2 - WATER DISHES – Water dishes provided with most crates are not suitable for travel due to their small size. We recommend you purchase plastic food containers. Purchase the size that permits two to be attached to the crate door. Cut two slits just below the lip about ½ - 1" from the end depending on the container size. Insert one zip tie into each slit. Fill with water to just below the zip tie and freeze and attach to the crate door (ice cubes may also be used). This provides constant hydration for your pet without filling its bladder early in the flight and also prevents water from spilling during take off or landing. If your pet chews, for their safety, it is best to purchase aluminum buckets and use the zip ties or clips to attach. If your pet is timid, you may add a burlap flap over the door opening to provide a more secure feeling.

3 - FLOORING/PADDING – We recommend (not required) that a piece of cardboard be placed in the bottom of the crate and then covered with lots of shredded paper to about 1/3rd full. This provides cushion as well as a consistently dry bed for the pets. If you choose to send a regular dog bed, please be advised that is must lie flat in the crate (no high sided beds due to security). If your pet is a chewer or you are unsure, do not use the shredded paper. You may also send blankets or towels – we suggest you handle the item(s) regularly and do not wash before shipment to give your pet the security of a familiar smell.

4 - VENTILATION – Crates must have ventilation on all four sides – most all airline approved crates have ventilation on each side and the front, so if you purchase a crate without vent holes on the back, ventilation holes must be drilled on the back.

5 - CRATE LABELING – Two red & white arrow labels should be placed on the RIGHT FRONT & LEFT REAR corners of the crate, and the yellow Live Animals on each UPPER side with the arrows pointing upward as well as one on the UPPER back of the crate (not pictured). Red & White identification & food & water label (not pictured) should be placed on the TOP of the crate, just above the door. Use additional sticky tape if necessary. Please indicate temperament on the back of the Pet ID tag and use zip tie to attach to the front door. The airline may place other signage on your crate.

6 - LEASH AND COLLAR (if applicable) – Take a zip lock baggie and a leash and collar for your pet, it will be taped to the top of the crate by cargo staff. It is very possible that the airlines will require you remove the pet from the crate for security inspection and measuring so be SURE that whomever is going to the airport has a means to secure the animal outside the crate. The airlines MUST provide a secure area to remove the pet so please insist on this if it is not offered.

7 - PROHIBITED ITEMS – high sided beds, water containers not attached to crate door, non solid toys

8 - MEDICATIONS – If your pet has meds, they must be in a prescription bottle. If the medication must be administered during any animal center layover, please clearly provide instructions for administration.

PAC MEASURING GUIDELINES
Courtesy of Pet Air Carrier 770-645-1837
www.petaircarrier.com pac@petaircarrier.com

Safe Pet Shipping Around The Globe

HOW TO MEASURE YOUR DOG

Proper kennel size is regulated by IATA (International Animal Transport Association); however, some airlines have more strict regulations. The crate must be large enough for your pet(s) to sit, stand, turn around & lie down without curling in the front legs. Brachyecephalic breeds (aka snub nose) will require one size larger than normally required for extra air flow.

A= length of animal from nose to base of tail (do not measure the tail)
B = height from ground to elbow joint
C = width across shoulders
D = height in relaxed standing position (top of head for pets with non-erect ears - to tip of ears for pets w/ erect ears)

The minimum length of the kennel must be equal to A + 1/2 B
The minimum width of the kennel must be equal to C+1 in x 2 and x 3 for two small pets
The minimum height of the kennel must be equal to D + 3 inches

*Inside kennel dimension does NOT include the doorway or side rims. Most crate dims include entire outside measurements

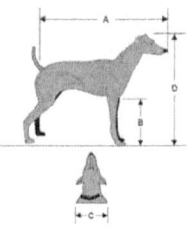

| Measuring guide | Plastic crate with extender | Breed restricted/oversize dog crate |

GENERAL AIRLINE CRATE REQUIREMENTS:

The crate must be solid and leak proof and made of fiberglass, metal, rigid plastics, weld metal mesh, solid wood or plywood. The crate cannot be collapsible or have wheels, and there should be no opening door on the top (wire crates & sherpa bags are not acceptable). If a wooden crate is used (required for restricted or oversize breeds) & mesh is used for ventilation, the wire mesh must be 16 gauge ¾ inch square

- Handling space bars or handles must be present on the long side of the crate.
- The container door must have a secure, spring loaded, all around locking system with the pins extending at least 1.6 cm (5/8 in) beyond the horizontal extrusions above and below the door. We strongly recommend the door be further secured with cable/zip ties at each corner.
- The door must be constructed of heavy plastic, welded or cast metal strong enough so that a pet cannot bend them and must be nose and paw proof so as not to injure your pet in any way.
- All crates must have two water containers attached to the front door.
- 3 – 5" extenders can be added to XL and giant crates if your pet(s) meet the length requirement but do not meet the height requirement (pictured above). This is typically less expensive than moving to the next size crate as all airfreight is based on crate size.

Please contact us at 770-645-1837 or via email at pac@petaircarrier.com if you have any questions regarding your crate purchase. If you provide the proper measurements for your pet(s), PAC can drop ship a crate to you for convenience, or we can advise you where you can purchase for yourself. If size is questionable to you, it is also best to take your pet to a local pet store and send us photos of your pet(s) in and beside the crate.

APPENDIX 2 - TRAVELING WITH DOGS BY AIR AND BY SEA

CHECKLIST Traveling with Dogs

DOWNLOAD THESE PDFS at WWW.NAVIGATECONTENT.COM

Created by Michelle Segrest

Navigate Content

(information accurate as of August 2018)

LEGAL REQUIREMENTS FOR DOGS

	FEES	MICRO CHIP	RABIES	VET HEALTH CERTIFICATE	QUARANTINE	IMPORT PERMIT	HEARTWORM, LEISHMANIASIS, NIPAH VIRUS AND/OR HENDRA VIRUS	TAPEWORMS and TICKS and FLEAS	APP FORM	OTHER
Aruba		✓	30 days prior to arrival	14 days prior to arrival						
Bahamas	$10 each plus $5 fax fee (money order or cash)		Not less than 1 month, not more than 10 months prior	Presented within 48 hours of arrival to licensed vet for examination		Ministry of Agriculture, Trade and Industry (Nassau).				
Barbados	Submit app form with BDS$25 each to Veterinary Services Dept. money order or certified bank draft only to The Permanent Secretary, Ministry of Agriculture US$15 processing fee Entry fee BDS $60 each	✓	At least 35 days prior	Endorsed by an Official Government/Federal Veterinarian (USDA in USA).			✓	Within 7 days of departure		notify Veterinary Services at least three (3) business days notice in advance of your arrival date/time
Belgium		✓	Within 10 days of departure	Within 10 days of departure						EU Pet Passport
Bermuda	Import duty, up to 25% of animal's true value.	✓	Within last 6 months	Within 10 days of arrival Name, date of birth, breed, description and microchip identification of pet; Owner at present; Owner in Bermuda and address.		✓		✓		rabies vaccination history, showing at least two rabies vaccinations, and that all rabies vaccinations have been given by a licensed veterinarian. The most recent vaccination was given at least 30 days, and not more than 12 months prior to arrival

77

	FEES	MICRO CHIP	RABIES	VET HEALTH CERTIFICATE	QUARANTINE	IMPORT PERMIT	HEARTWORM, LEISHMANIASIS, NIPAH VIRUS AND/OR HENDRA VIRUS	TAPEWORMS and TICKS and FLEAS	APP FORM	OTHER
Denmark		✓	21 days prior to travel	Endorsed by USDA					✓	
Domin. Republic			✓	certified by the Agriculture Department of your State and Apostilled by the State Government			30 days prior to departure	30 days prior to departure		
France		✓	At least 21 days prior	Endorsed by USDA Valid for 10 days						
Germany		✓	✓	✓						Declaration in writing (see pdf) stating that the pet travel is not intended for sale or a change of hands.
Guadaloupe			Endorse by USDA							
Morocco			Within 6 months	10 days prior to departure						
Netherlands		✓	✓	Valid for 10 days only						
Portugal	50,00 € for vet exam at point of entry	✓	✓							Travellers' Points of Entry (e.g. Airports). You will need to contact the point of entry you plan to travel to and notify them of your arrival at least 48 hours prior. See the attached forms
Puerto Rico			✓							Tag with name and contact info
Spain		✓		In Spanish and English						
Turks and Caicos	$50 per animal			✓		import application (pdf). must be submitted and approved at least one week prior to travel.				

	FEES	MICRO CHIP	RABIES	VET HEALTH CERTIFICATE	QUARANTINE	IMPORT PERMIT	HEARTWORM, LEISHMANIASIS, NIPAH VIRUS AND/OR HENDRA VIRUS	TAPEWORMS and TICKS and FLEAS	APP FORM	OTHER
UK		✓	At least 21 days prior	Obtain an **official third country veterinary certificate**. Contact your local USDA accredited veterinarian to obtain the APHIS 7001 Health Certificate.				Tapeworm treatment must be administered by a vet not less than 24 hours and not more than 120 hours (1-5 days) before arrival time in the UK.		
USA			30 days prior to entry	✓						
US Virgin Islands			Within 6 months prior	✓						
British Virgin Islands	$10 USD per animal									

GENERAL GUIDELINES & REGULATIONS

In general, when sailing with dogs you need three key items:

1. **USDA-stamped health certificate**. This must be approved by a licensed veterinarian, then shipped to the state's health department for signature and seal. This must happen within 10 days of the flight. For us, we had to ship the certificate overnight to Montgomery, Alabama, and have it returned to us before we left for our flight to Frankfurt.
2. **International microchip.**
3. **Rabies vaccination** AFTER the microchip has been implanted.

7 TIPS FOR LONG-DISTANCE CRUISING

FROM THE ARTICLE: **HOW TO GO LONG DISTANCE CRUISING WITH YOUR DOG OR CAT** (Bunting, 2015)

- ☐ The dog will learn to do his business on board, even if it takes a few days. No worries.
- ☐ Stock up on food when you have the chance.
- ☐ Have some games for the dog so that they don't get bored on the boat. You will have fewer opportunities to walk/exercise your dog than at home, regardless of the trips to the beach. We played "kick it and find it"– kick it is when the dog sits at the top of the steps and kicks a ball down the stairs for me to catch and throw back to him. Find it is where I conceal a ball somewhere on the boat for the dog to find and return it.

- Bringing any pet on a boat requires internet research. A really helpful site is www.pettravel.com. They sell documents, but most documents can be found online at no cost. Search for Department of Agriculture and Pet Import Permit.
- In the Caribbean:
    - In Saint Lucia many locals are afraid of dogs or don't like dogs.
    - On the other hand, dogs seem to be very welcome in French islands such as Martinique, Guadeloupe, etc. People here seem to like dogs, and it is no problem to take a dog to a restaurant.
    - Any non-French island: never bring a dog to a restaurant.
    - Avoid beaches with people as a courtesy.
    - Do not take a dog to national park beaches, such as St. Thomas or the U.S. Virgin Islands.
- So far, no vet has checked the microchip. We wouldn't recommend going without it, though.

REQUIREMENTS BY COUNTRY

These are the countries we researched before August 2018. Please use the links provided to obtain current information, requirements, and application forms. All this information was gathered from published articles, from individual country websites, and from www.bringfido.com, www.noonsite.com, www.petfriendlytravel.com, and www.pettravel.com. Please remember that it is important to follow the links provided to obtain the most current information before you travel internationally with your pet. Please also remember that our research was for dogs originating from the United States. If your country of origin is not the U.S., these requirements may be different.

EUROPE

Every European country has different rules. However, in Europe it is easier to travel with dogs because there is a European Pet Passport that is valid throughout the European Union with the exception of the U.K. There is still a lot of additional work to do, though—with the paperwork and expense of vaccines, antibiotics, and veterinarian inspections.

UNITED KINGDOM

The United Kingdom will not allow you to enter its ports with a dog from the U.S. on a private vessel. Period. This may be true of dogs from other origins, as well. We had to avoid the U.K. altogether. With the proper paperwork, you can enter with dogs on an airplane or ferry, and in some cases by going to Ireland first, but not on a private vessel.

ARUBA

In order to travel with your pet to Aruba, you will only need a Veterinary Health Certificate issued from the originating country no more than 14 days prior to arrival, and you will need a rabies inoculation certificate issued within 30 days prior to arrival. Your pet will also need a microchip prior to traveling to Aruba. Be advised: the dog or cat must have lived continuously in a country with a low percentage of rabies for six months preceding the travel date or must have been born and have lived in the country of birth continuously until the date of travel. Pets may not enter Aruba from any country with a high percentage of rabies.

BELGIUM

Your pet must have a microchip, or a tattoo (as long as it was given before July 3, 2011 and is still readable). Within 10 days before your departure to Belgium, you must go to your vet to get an international health certificate. Be sure it includes proof of a valid vaccination from rabies. If you plan to travel within Europe upon your arrival to Belgium, you will need to get an EU Pet Passport from a vet in Belgium.

BELIZE

When you enter the country, the pet animal is to be accompanied by a veterinary certificate issued by a registered veterinarian in the country of origin, stating that the pet animal is clinically healthy, free of signs of infectious and contagious disease, free of ticks, and has no fresh wound or wound in the process of healing. The certificate must also show that the pet animal has been vaccinated against rabies and that its vaccination is current. The date of vaccination and the name of the vaccine manufacturer must be indicated on the certificate. If your pet is less than four months old and cannot receive the rabies vaccination, they will need to be house quarantined until 30 days after rabies vaccination by a registered veterinarian. All pet animals entering Belize are to be inspected by a Belize Agricultural Health Authority (BAHA) official. Pet animals from countries affected with diseases and pests of quarantine importance (FMD, screwworm, etc.) will require veterinary inspection at port of entry. You will be informed of the need for veterinary inspection when permit is issued. Be sure to notify BAHA of the date and time of arrival, and your flight number, two days before you and your pet arrive to ensure that a veterinary officer is present at the time of entry. All costs of quarantine will be your responsibility. Make sure the cage is new or cleaned and disinfected prior to use for the transportation of your pet. While it is not required, BAHA strongly suggests that all dogs be vaccinated against distemper, hepatitis, leptospirosis and parvovirus, and all cats be vaccinated against feline viral rhinotracheitis, calici virus, and panleucopenia. Lastly, your pet should be treated against endoparasites and ectoparasites within 30 days of departure from Belize.

BRAZIL

You will require an international health certificate for animals (Certificado Zoosanitário Internacional -CZI). The certificate must be issued by a licensed veterinarian 10 days before departure and must show no disease present. The certificate must also confirm that no incidence of contagious disease has been detected in the place of origin up to 40 days before departure. A certificate of vaccination against rabies for any animal over 90 days old (obtained 30 days before entry in the case of animals vaccinated for the first time). This must be valid for at least one year. Please provide proof of owner's full name and address, including state and country. You must provide documents showing the animal's name, breed, gender, size, color, coat, and any other specific markings. Copies of all relevant documents are required for animals imported as cargo. The same requirements apply to guide dogs. Birds are prohibited.

COLOMBIA

Your pet will need a Health Certificate issued by your local veterinarian at least 8 days prior to travel to Colombia. The certificate must specify: species, ID, breed, gender, age, and type. It should also state that the animal was found free of contagious and parasitic diseases, that it doesn't have any fresh or healing wounds, that it has a valid and current vaccination plan, and that it is suitable for transport. Make sure to notify officials if the animal was treated with internal or external antiparasitic products whose use is duly authorized in the exporting country. Once your pet is confirmed healthy and the documentation of the animal had been verified, the ICA will issue the Sanitary Inspection Certificate (SIC), whose fee has been established previously by the ICA. Staffordshire Terrier, Pit Bull Terrier, American Pit Bull Terrier, and crosses or hybrids of these breeds are strictly prohibited from entering Colombia.

COSTA RICA

You will need to have your pet examined within 30 days of departure. The pet must be found healthy and free of any clinical signs of infectious disease. If you are traveling with a dog, you must show proof they were vaccinated against distemper, hepatitis, leptospirosis, parvovirus, and rabies. If you are traveling with a cat, you must show proof they were vaccinated against rabies. Pets over three months of age must be vaccinated against rabies. The rabies vaccine must be applied a minimum of 30 days before arrival. You will need to have a veterinarian complete two copies of the International Health Certificate (PDF link below). An official rabies vaccination certificate must accompany the health documents and is valid for the period of the vaccine (1 or 3 years). Pets can enter Costa Rica either with the owner either in-cabin or as "baggage" on the same flight. Depending upon the length of stay, pets entering Costa Rica from the U.S. may or may not need additional documentation in order to leave Costa Rica and return to the US. If the pet enters Costa Rica and stays longer than the validity of the U.S. Health Certificate (30 days for APHIS Form 7001), then that pet will need a valid Costa Rican Health Certificate in order to leave. If the pet leaves during the time period of the validity of the U.S. Health Certificate, then that is all that is required to leave Costa Rica—if the pet leaves with the same person with whom it entered AND is returning to the same city in the U.S. If that is not the case, then the pet will require a new Costa Rican Health Certificate in order to leave.

DENMARK

You will need to complete and carry a copy of the Authorization Form (PDF link below). Your pet must have a valid microchip or a clearly readable tattoo applied before July 3, 2011. You will need a Health Certificate from your veterinarian and have it endorsed by the USDA. Your pet must be at least 12 weeks old and cannot be vaccinated prior to receiving their microchip. The vaccine needs to be given at least 21 days prior to traveling to Denmark. If your trip is longer that four weeks, your dog must be registered in the Danish Dog Register upon arrival. There are several breeds that are not allowed entry into Denmark, including: Pit Bull Terrier, Tosa Inu, American Staffordshire Terrier, Fila Brasileiro, Dogo Argentino,

American Bulldog, Boerboel, Kangal, Central Asian Shepherd Dog (ovtcharka), Caucasian Shepherd Dog (ovtcharka), South Russian Shepherd Dog (ovtcharka), Tornjak and Sarplaninac. Cross-breeds of any of the breeds mentioned above are also not allowed in Denmark, and there are no exceptions. However, if you did own your dog prior to March 17, 2010, the dog will be covered by the transitional arrangements.

FRANCE

The animal must be at least 12 weeks old. Your pet must be identified by a microchip (standard ISO 11784 or annex A ISO standard 11785) or a tattoo. In case of identification with a tattoo, the tattoo must be clearly readable and applied before July 2011. Your pet must have a valid rabies vaccination. If it is the first rabies vaccination for your pet, you must wait 21 days between the last shot of the vaccination and departure. You must get a health certificate from your veterinarian, endorsed by the USDA. USDA endorsement is required for all certificates except those issued by military veterinarians for dogs, cats, and ferrets. The official health certificate will be valid for 10 days from the date of endorsement by the USDA until the date of arrival into France. The following breeds are forbidden to travel into France unless they are registered by the American Kennel Club under special rules: Staffordshire terrier, American Staffordshire terrier (pitbulls), Mastiff (boerbulls), Rottweilers, and Tosa.

GERMANY

Your pets will need to be identified by either a clearly readable tattoo or by a microchip. Proof of valid immunization against rabies must be recorded in the animal health certificate (link to PDF below). Pets must be vaccinated against rabies at least 21 days before traveling to Germany. You can only enter Germany with a pet if you are the owner or a designated person is responsible for them. You must provide a declaration in writing stating that the pet travel is not intended for sale or a change of hands. Puppies and kittens are not allowed entry into Germany if they are under 15 weeks old.

GUADELOUPE

Pets are able to enter Guadeloupe with proof of a rabies vaccination certificate, signed by a licensed veterinarian and valid in the United States (USDA). If the animal has never undergone a rabies vaccination or if the last date for the rabies booster has passed, it is mandatory to vaccinate or re-vaccinate your pet no less than 30 days before departure. Keep in mind: each family is limited to three animals, only one of which can be a puppy or a kitten (under six months of age), and a rabies vaccination of a young animal before three months of age is not recognized as valid.

JAMAICA

Only pets from Great Britain, Northern Ireland, and the Republic of Eire are allowed entry into Jamaica. See the website for more details.

MOROCCO

Ten days prior to departure, you will need to obtain a veterinarian good health certificate from the country of origin (USDA if in the U.S.). You will also need to get an anti-rabies certificate, issued within the last six months. We were actually able to use our European Pet Passport as a legal document and had no trouble with the check-in procedure for the dogs.

NETHERLANDS

Your pet must be identified with a microchip. Your pet must be vaccinated against rabies after being microchipped. If it is the first time that your pet gets the rabies vaccination after being microchipped, be aware that the rabies vaccination should be given at least 21 days before the pet's departure date to the Netherlands. Dogs and cats must be at least 15 weeks old in order to travel to the Netherlands. Your pet must also travel with a veterinarian health certificate from an accredited vet. After the certificate has been signed by the vet, it is valid for 10 days for entry into the Netherlands.

NICARAGUA

Before you arrive, you will only need a health certificate (preferably issued by the USDA. However, health certificates issued by your local veterinarian showing proof of a recent rabies vaccine and proof of a parasite treatment within the past year are acceptable). When you arrive in Nicaragua, you will need to pay $10USD per pet to a MAGFOR Quarantine Delegate at the Managua International Airport. You will also need to pay an additional $10USD per pet to customs. It is recommended that you ask for assistance from airline personnel to contact the MAGFOR Quarantine Delegate; their office is near the immigration check points. The MAGFOR Quarantine Delegate will require the original form of the certificate and any other documentation you have brought.

PANAMA

If you are bringing pets to Panama, be sure to complete the entry requirements below:
You will need to have the Form 7001 filled out and certified by an official USDA Veterinary and your pet's veterinarian. The Consular Fee is $30.00 per document, payable by money order made out to the Consulate of Panama. You must include a self-addressed, prepaid envelope for return of documents. Fill out the Home Quarantine Request. The fee for the Home Quarantine is B/.130.00°° per pet paid only in cash at Tocumen Airport. Upon arrival at the Tocumen Airport, all documents have to be given to the veterinary doctor of the Department of Zoonosis Control. Your pet will be returned to you as long as you provide the required documentation. If you do not provide the required documentation, your pet will be returned back to the country of origin.

PORTUGAL

Your pet will need to have a microchip. You will need an international health certificate, which you can get from your local veterinarian. You will need to provide proof of anti-rabies vaccination (vaccination record or other). Animals are checked in places called Travelers' Points of Entry (e.g., airports). You will need to contact the point of entry you plan to travel to and notify them of your arrival at least 48 hours prior. An entry fee is required following the Veterinary Expert Examination that is carried out at Travelers' Points of Entry when pets are checked: one animal 30,00 €; two or more animals 50,00 €. Portugal has additional requirements if your dog is considered a "dangerous" breed. Go to this link for more information regarding additional documentation: http://www.dgv.min-agricultura.pt/portal/page/portal/DGV/genericos?generico=9846601&cboui=9846601.

PUERTO RICO

The requirements to bring pets to Puerto Rico are simple. Just be sure to have a tag with name of the pet and your contact information, as well as a rabies quarantine certificate from your local veterinarian stating that the pet has had a rabies shot.

SPAIN

First, pets should be accompanied by their owners or representatives. Second, your pet must be identified with a legible tattoo or microchip, and third, they need to have their animal health certificate. Be sure a copy of the health certificate is also completed in Spanish. Dogs and cats that are less than three months old are not allowed entry due to their inability to receive the rabies vaccine. Pets must not travel within 21 days after their first vaccination.

TRINIDAD AND TOBAGO

In order for you to travel with your pet to Trinidad and Tobago, first you will need to apply for an import permit. Application forms can be obtained from the Animal Production and Health Division. One form of valid identification is to be presented (passport, ID card, or driver's permit) upon application along with the letter of authorization (if applicable). You will need to apply for a health certificate from the USDA (for U.S. travelers). Lastly, be sure to contact the Veterinary Office to provide flight/landing information 28 to 48 hours in advance of your arrival.

TURKS AND CAICOS

You must provide a valid veterinary certificate from your country of origin. If this document is not in English, it must be translated and notarized. Complete the import application (link to PDF below). It must be submitted and approved at least one week prior to travel. A fee of $50 must be paid upon arrival in Turks and Caicos (per animal). The following breeds are prohibited from entry into the islands: Akita, any breed of bulldog, any breed of mastiff, American Staffordshire Terrier, Pit Bull Terrier, the Staffordshire Bull Terrier, and any mixed-breed dog which has any Pit Bull lineage, Bandog, Beauceron, Canary dog, or Presa Canario, Doberman Pinscher, Dogo Argentino, Fila Brazilliero, Japanese Tosa, Jindo, Kuvasz, Rhodesian Ridgeback, Roman Fighting Dog Rottweiler, South African Boerboel, or any dog which appears to have been bred for fighting.

UNITED STATES

The CDC does not require general certificates of health for pets for entry into the United States. However, health certificates may be required for entry into some states, or may be required by airlines for pets. You should check with officials in your destination state and with your airline prior to the travel date. Dogs are subject to inspection at ports of entry and may be denied entry into the United States if they have evidence of an infectious disease that can be transmitted to humans. If a dog appears to be ill, further examination by a licensed veterinarian at the owner's expense might be required at the port of entry. You must provide proof of rabies vaccination: Dogs must have a certificate showing they have been vaccinated against rabies at least 30 days prior to entry in the United States. These requirements apply to both pets and service animals.

Importation of Dogs from Rabies-Free Countries: Unvaccinated dogs may be imported without proof of a rabies vaccination if they have been located in a country that's free of rabies for at least six months. Following importation, all dogs are subject to state and local vaccination or health certificate requirements.

U.S. VIRGIN ISLANDS

Pets just need to have an official health certificate stating that they did not originate from an area quarantined for rabies. Your pet must have been vaccinated for rabies within six months prior to the date of travel except those pets less than 12 weeks old. The certificate of vaccination for rabies must be attached to the official health certificate. No import permit is required.

EASTERN CARIBBEAN

The following information was obtained from this article:
CRUISING THE EASTERN CARIBBEAN WITH YOUR DOG: SOMETIMES CHALLENGING, OFTEN POSSIBLE (Liesbet).

However, it also includes information from **BRING FIDO** (Bring Fido, n.d.), **PET TRAVEL** (Pet Travel, n.d.), and **NOON SITE** (Noon Site, n.d.).

> *If you think Eastern Caribbean check-in procedures are inconsistent, different on every island, time consuming, annoying, and sometimes costly, try doing it with a dog…*
>
> *We human beings can visit any country in the Caribbean without proving our health, but our totally healthy pets (who would want to have a rabid dog on their boat?) need health records, up-to-date vaccinations, microchips, and health certificates. To be able to experience the Caribbean with our four-legged friends, and do it legally, as required by all the different islands, cruisers have to put up with a lot of hassle, frustration, misinformation, time commitment, and fees, and show a high level of endurance on top of it all. But it is possible!*
>
> *With the following overview we will try to inform you about the check-in procedures for your dog in the Eastern Caribbean islands. This information is based on correspondence with government officials and agriculture departments, online*

regulations, and our own experience. It will give you an idea about what cruising the Caribbean with your dog involves and hopefully will make things easier when checking into the countries.

BAHAMAS

For entry into The Bahamas, new one-year rabies vaccinations, import permit applications, and required documents should be emailed in advance to the Saint Lucia and Bahamas authorities. An import permit is required from the Ministry of Agriculture, Trade and Industry (Nassau), for all animals being brought into The Bahamas. Applications for such permits (along with a $10 processing fee) must be made in writing to the Director of Agriculture, Ministry of Agriculture, Trade and Industry, PO Box N-3704, Nassau, The Bahamas. For more information, call 242-325-7502 or 242-325-7509. The application must be accompanied by a $10 processing fee for each animal and a $5 fax fee in cases where persons wish to have the permit faxed to them. They accept money order or cash only; no personal checks are accepted. If you're coming from the U.S. and Canada, the following are the main provisions of the import permit as it applies to dogs and cats: The animal must be six months of age or older. The animal must be accompanied by a valid certificate which substantiates that it has been vaccinated against rabies within not less than one month and not more than 10 months prior to importation for the one-year vaccine. For the three-year vaccine, it must have been administered between no less than one month and no more than 34 months prior to importation into The Bahamas. The animal must be accompanied by a Veterinary Health Certificate presented within 48 hours of arrival in the Commonwealth of The Bahamas to a licensed veterinarian for an examination. The permit is valid for one entry and must be used within one year from the date of issue. Regulations for all other types of animals and relating to countries not mentioned above may be obtained from the Director of Agriculture, PO Box N-3704, Nassau, The Bahamas. Applications should state the kind of animal, breed, sex, age, and country of embarkation. Additional information may be required if, for example, the animal is listed under the Convention on International Trade in Endangered Species of Wild Plants and Animals (CITES). Customs duty for permanent entry of all animals from outside the Commonwealth of The Bahamas (dogs, cats, cattle, and horses) is $10, plus 1/2% of the value of the animal. Yearly fees for dog licenses in New Providence, Grand Bahama, and the Family Islands are $2 for males or spayed females and $6 for unspayed females. Animals not meeting these requirements will not be allowed to enter the Commonwealth of The Bahamas. Commonwealth of The Bahamas ($10 USD per animal plus $5 fax fee) accepts cash only.

FOR MORE ABOUT BAHAMAS ENTRY READ THIS ARTICLE FROM THE BOAT GALLEY (Shearlock, Getting a Bahamas Pet Permit, 2016)

BARBADOS

If you bring your cat and dog on a private boat, you will not be allowed to tie up on any pier/dock in Barbados. You will only be allowed to tie up for outfitting the vessel, e.g., water, fuel. Your animals will not be allowed to land without the proper paperwork and permits. *Website:* http://agriculture.gov.bb
Requirements: Dog has to be imported directly from the United Kingdom, Ireland, Australia or New Zealand OR must have been living continuously for six months in Antigua & Barbuda, St. Kitts & Nevis, St. Vincent, St. Lucia or Jamaica prior to entering Barbados. *Procedure:* Complete an application form (available online), pay the fee, give three days' notice of the dog's expected arrival date, along with transportation information, import permit

number, name, address and contact information pet owner and name and information customs broker.
Fee: US$ 12.5 (BDS$ 25) permit fee. US$ 30 (BDS$ 60) landing fee Your pet must have a microchip. The implantation must be done before the rabies vaccination. After your pet has been microchipped, it must be vaccinated against rabies. After your pet is vaccinated, you must wait 35 days before your trip to Barbados. Your pet will need to be tested for heartworm, leishmaniasis, nipah virus and/or hendra virus if such viruses are present in your country. Your veterinarian can have these tests done and, once the results are negative, your pet is free to travel. If your pet is a dog, it should be treated by for tapeworms and ticks by a veterinarian within seven days of scheduled departure for Barbados. Once you've completed the requirements, your pet will be issued with an Official Export Health Certificate, which must be endorsed by an official government or federal veterinarian (USDA in the U.S.). Once your pet meets the conditions for import into Barbados, download and complete an application form (link to PDF below). Submit the application form along with a BDS$25 to the Veterinary Services Department. Payment may be made by money order or certified bank draft only to The Permanent Secretary, Ministry of Agriculture. The bank draft or money order must be in United States currency for the amount of US$15.00 (to cover all additional bank processing charges). You must notify Veterinary Services at least three business days in advance of your arrival date/time and flight information. You will also need to include your import permit number, name, local address, and contact information, and the name and contact information of the customs broker. If there are any changes, notify Veterinary Services as soon as possible. Pets must travel as manifested cargo and can be received at the Animal Reception Centre. A landing certificate is issued when the pet is cleared for entry into Barbados. Fees for dogs and cats are BDS $60 per animal. Fees are payable for Landing Certificates of ALL animals. They are due at the time of examination at the port of entry. Customs duties are collected on any non-livestock animals imported into Barbados. In order to facilitate the process, you will need to work with a customs broker. If you do not, it will cause serious delays in receiving your pet. If your pet is only visiting and will be returning to its country of origin, customs duties may be refundable at the time of departure. Contact your customs broker for further information. Upon receipt of the application and fee, a permit will be prepared and forwarded to you either by mail, fax, or email. Animal import permits are valid for six months from the date of issue. When the animal arrives in Barbados, it will be taken directly from the airline to the Animal Reception Centre, where it will be inspected by a veterinary officer. As long as all terms of the import permit are met and the veterinary inspection fee has been paid and your pet is found healthy, the landing certificate fee will be issued. Keep in mind: overtime charges will apply if your pet arrives outside of standard government working hours (Monday to Friday, 8:15 a.m. to 4:30 p.m.), weekends, and public holidays.

BERMUDA

Bermuda will only accept rabies vaccinations that were given within the previous 10 months. Your pet must have a microchip. You will need to get a veterinary health certificate issued within 10 days before your arrival in Bermuda, stating that the animal is not infected with any communicable disease and is free of external parasites. The veterinary health certificate must contain the following information: name, date of birth, breed, description, and microchip identification of pet; owner at present; owner in Bermuda and owner's local address. The veterinarian needs to write a note stating that the pet has been treated on the day of examination with a flea and tick repellent. See the website for acceptable treatments. You will also need a veterinary statement that your pet has not been exposed to rabies nor been present in an officially quarantined rabies area within the last six months. Get a copy of your pet's rabies vaccination history, showing at least two rabies vaccinations and that all rabies vaccinations have been given by a licensed veterinarian and are in accord with all of these requirements. Also show that the most recent vaccination was given at least 30 days, and not more than 12 months, prior to arrival in Bermuda. Dogs and cats under the age of 10 months, and dogs and cats of any age that have received only a single rabies vaccination, will not be allowed into Bermuda. The faxed or emailed copy of the import permit and the original veterinary certificates must accompany the animal on arrival. Import permits are only valid for 10 days from the date of the veterinary certificate. Pets may be subject to a Customs import duty, up to 25% of their true value. Duty is payable to Bermuda Customs at the port of entry, at the time of the animal's arrival.

U.S. VIRGIN ISLANDS

Just like in the United States and Puerto Rico, it is very easy to visit the USVI with your dog. There is a check box on the customs form and the officer may ask a few questions. Be sure to bring your dog's paperwork, just in case he/she needs to see the vaccination records. You should have a Rabies Certificate that is less than three years old.

BRITISH VIRGIN ISLANDS

Website: http://www.bvi.gov.vg/content/dog-license-registration *Requirements:* Microchip, Government Health Certificate, Rabies Certificate (1 year or newer), DHCCP Certificate, Titer Certificate. *Procedure:* Fill out application obtained via email or fax with tentative date and time of arrival. Fax Application, Government Health Certificate, Rabies Certificate, DHCCP Certificate, and Titer Certificate. Ideally, all the documents state the dog's microchip. Dog must be checked in at West End or Road Town in Tortola. The morning you depart port for Tortola, call 1-284-468-9693 or 1-284-468-9243 to let them know a more specific date and time of arrival. Bring yourself and your pet to customs. An officer will meet you there, inspect the animal, read the microchip, look through the documents, collect the fee, and issue the import permit. *Fee:* US$ 10 per dog. *Our Experience:* We emailed back and forth multiple times, but the important communication had to be done by fax. They need a fax number to send the conditions and application form. They faxed us an application, we filled it out, and we sent it back. They would fax an import permit back to us, but we preferred that the vet who would examine our dogs would bring the permit with him in West End. The inspecting vets are friendly, efficient and professional. The official regulations state more requirements, but the above-mentioned ones seem sufficient. We did get questioned about only having one instead of two titer (serological) tests done and about the fact that our titer is older than 12 months. We proved that our dogs were healthy and stressed the fact that it is very hard to obtain extra titer certificates from the Caribbean (blood samples can only be sent to and tested in two places in the whole world: one in the U.K. and one in Kansas, USA). As long as the dog has subsequent rabies shots to date, one titer certificate should do, according to the strict U.K. requirements we use as our "make-sense guidelines."

ST. MARTIN, ST. BARTH, MARTINIQUE

When checking in to these French islands, pets don't have to be declared. It is recommended that you have the dog's paperwork on board and that you act responsibly. We have found that many beaches have "no dogs" signs (not often enforced) and locals don't seem too pleased about or interested in pets (compared to the English-speaking islands). Many restaurants do allow a dog at your side, however.

ANGUILLA

Website: http://www.gov.ai/pets.htm. *Requirements:* Health Certificate, Rabies Certificate (1 year or newer) *Procedure:* Apply for an import permit for your dog by phone. The permit is filled out over the phone, signed by the vet, and faxed to you. Once in Anguilla, take the permit and health certificate to the port of entry. The permit must then be paid for at the Agriculture Department in The Village (on the road to Crocus Bay). *Fee:* US$ 16 (EC$ 40) *Experience:* We did not make any preparations and only planned on spending two nights in Road Bay if all worked out ok. We tried to contact the government vet multiple times, without success, and ended up explaining our predicament (of not getting a response and a dog that needed to relief himself) to customs. We promised to never take him beyond the beach and received a reluctant "go ahead" until we got in touch with the government vet, which never happened during our brief visit. *Remarks:* The government of Anguilla is very strict about Import Permits, so it is highly recommended that you get in touch with them before arrival. Persistence is required in getting through to the office.

SABA, STATIA, ST. MAARTEN

Recommended: Current Health Certificate, Rabies Certificate, dog's paperwork. *Procedure:* Pets do not have to be declared on the customs form. *Experience:* Before we arrived in Statia, the Director of Tourism of Saba, Glenn Holm, replied to my inquiry as follows: "There's a great chance you won't even be checked or asked for the documentation but it's always good to have it on hand just in case you are asked." He indicated that the rules are the same for both sister islands. *Remarks:* Emailing with Glenn Holm was a pleasant experience, and we encountered no problems whatsoever taking our dog ashore in Statia and St. Maarten.

ST. KITTS AND NEVIS

Requirements: Rabies Certificate, Titer Certificate, Health Certificate *Procedure:* Email or fax the dog's documents with an idea of the date and time of the ship's arrival. In the port of entry, a vet will inspect the animal and issue an import permit. *Fee:* US$ 40 (EC $ 100) weekdays from 8 a.m. - 4 p.m. US$ 50 (EC$ 125) after 4 p.m. and on weekends. *Experience:* Information online is inadequate. (doastk@sisterisles.kn never responds or its mailbox is full), communication with the government vets ranges from nonexistent (many unanswered inquiries) to confusing and nonclarifying. After emailing the required documents and not hearing anything back, we decided to show up in Basseterre with our dog. Nobody at customs knew what to do, the vets were unreachable or busy for at least 24 hours, and everything was a huge hassle and mystery while our dog was not allowed on shore. We decided to move the boat to a more remote area during our visit in these islands. *Remarks:* Good luck with this one! Inefficiency and lack of communication make it hard for a cruising pet owner to do the right thing in order to visit this country. If you need some assistance, Akela Browne of the St. Kitts Tourism Bureau in Basseterre (akela.browne@stkittstourism.kn) proved helpful in one instance.

MONTSERRAT

Requirements: Rabies Certificate, Titer Certificate, DHCCP Certificate, list of all ports visited in the six weeks prior to arrival in Montserrat, proof of treatment for internal and external parasites (between 3-7 days before arrival), Health Certificate from previously visited country. *Procedure:* Email or fax the required health documents with the list of visited ports. Inform the veterinary officer of the date and approximate time of arrival at least 48 hours prior to anchoring. Upon checking in, inform the customs officer about the dog aboard, and a government vet will inspect the animal and make a final decision on its entry (and more than likely hands you an import permit). *Fee:* Free. *Experience:* Correspondence with the vet department went smooth and the inspection was short and efficient. No questions were asked and no more documents needed to be shown. We treat our dog monthly for parasites but were not asked for proof. We did not have a health certificate from St. Kitts and Nevis (the previously visited country), but when we explained why, they accepted our health certificate from St. Maarten. *Remarks:* Temporarily importing your dog in Montserrat can be done efficiently, painlessly, and in a timely manner. Dr. Waldron and Dr. Maloney were prompt and courteous with their responses and inspection.

ANTIGUA AND BARBUDA

Requirements: Microchip, Rabies Certificate (newer than 1 year), Titer Certificate, Lyme Disease Test (less than six months old), medical and vaccination history, Government Health Certificate (newer than seven days), proof of treatment for internal and external parasites (within seven days before arrival) *Procedure:* Fax or email the information required to start the import license process. After the documents have been reviewed, an import license can be issued upon arrival. Inform the Veterinary Division of the date and time of arrival at least 48 hours ahead of time and contact them (let them know you need a Lyme Disease Test, if needed) upon check-in. A government vet will come inspect the animal and the documents. If you don't have a Lyme Disease Certificate, the test can be done upon arrival for the equivalent of US$ 41 (EC$ 11 0). *Fee:* US$ 50 or EC$ 130 for the inspection *Experience:* Before we arrived in Antigua, we never found out about the fees (they are mentioned on the website now) and we didn't have a Lyme Disease test. Our boat had to be tied on the quarantine dock in Jolly Harbour before we were allowed to check ourselves in with a dog. Check on this procedure in English/Falmouth Harbour. We were prepared to obtain the Lyme Disease test here if the fee was reasonable. After four hours of waiting, the vet arrived. Before agreeing to do anything else, we wanted to know the fees. They were not reasonable. It would cost us over US $90 just for the dog to be able to legally visit Antigua and Barbuda. Add the fee for a cruising permit and the cost was just too high for us, "poor" budget cruisers. We decided against paying and therefore visiting these islands. We explained the situation to Customs and Immigration and told them it was too late and we were too tired to continue our trip to Guadeloupe. We obtained permission to spend the night in Jolly Harbour after paying for the cruising permit and were told to keep the dog on board. *Remarks:* If you are willing to pay the high fees, visiting Antigua and Barbuda with your dog is possible after declaring the animal in Antigua. Maybe check the price of the Lyme Disease test in a different country first to save some money. The rules are straightforward and the vets are efficient. Communication seems to have improved as well.

DOMINICA

Requirements: Health Certificate, DHCCP Certificate, Rabies Certificate (newer than 1 year), Titer Certificate, proof of treatment for parasites *Procedure:* Fax or email the dog's paperwork and health certificate. If all is in order, an import permit will be faxed/emailed back to you after the documents have been reviewed. Show this import permit when you check in. *Fee:* Free *Experience:* Communication with the vet department and obtaining the import permit are easy and straightforward (and free!). The permit is valid for one month. After the custom's officer saw our printed permit, all was ok the first time we visited Dominica in 2009, but now the Customs Department insists you call the government vet for an inspection before landing the dog. The numbers on the permit were invalid or remained unanswered when we tried multiple times, so we sent our contact another email to clarify the matter. So far, no inspection is needed to land your dog in Dominica; a valid import permit is enough. *Remarks:* Dominica is an easy place to temporarily import your dog, but be prepared to ignore the customs officer when asked to call the vet before landing your dog.

ST. LUCIA

Requirements: Microchip, Rabies Certificate (newer than 1 year), Titer Certificate (newer than 2 years), DHCCP Certificate, proof of treatment for parasites, Health Certificate *Procedure:* Fill out the application form for an import permit (available online) and email or fax it to the Agriculture Department, together with the dog's health records and an expected date of arrival. A current health certificate (ideally from the country previously visited) is required upon arrival. When arriving in St. Lucia, check in with customs, immigration and the port office (all in the same room in Rodney Bay) and call the vet office to arrange a time for one of the vets to come and inspect the dog, scan the microchip, bring a permit, and collect the fee. The dog is NOT allowed onshore without a permit. *Fee:* US $18 (EC$ 45) when applying for a permit ahead of time (preferred), US$26 (EC$ 65) when applying for the permit upon arrival (requires two vet visits). *Experience:* The email address available online has been having problems for a year. Checking your dog into St. Lucia is straightforward and easy in Rodney Bay.
Either you or the customs officer can call the Agriculture Department to set up a meeting with the vet. He will come to the marina/dock. *Remarks:* The best place to arrive in St. Lucia is Rodney Bay, where the process has been done by other cruisers many times before, customs can help with the phone number or a phone call, and the vet office is not too far away (towards Castries). Our experience in Soufriere was demotivating, expensive, and non-professional. It is advised to keep the permit with you each time you take your dog to shore. We have been asked for it by an immigration official walking around the Rodney Bay Marina area. Allowing foreign dogs into the country is a relatively new development in St. Lucia, so locals might ask you whether your dog is cleared, or they may wrongly tell you that your dog is not allowed in their country.

ST. VINCENT AND THE GRENADINES

Requirements: Microchip, Rabies Certificate, Titer Certificate, DHCCP Certificate, Government-Issued Export Health Certificate (important!), proof of treatment for parasites *Procedure:* Contact the vet department to obtain an application for an import permit. Fax or email the application with the dog's health records and an estimated date of arrival. Obtain a Government-Issued Health Certificate from the rabies-free country you are coming from (St. Lucia is the obvious choice. You will have to take your dog to the Department of Agriculture either by taxi, hitching a ride or private transportation). Sail to the south coast of St. Vincent, anchor or pick up a mooring at Young Island Cut. Remember that 48 hours' notice of arrival must be given. Once in Young Island Cut or another anchorage close by, call the vet department to set up an appointment. Meet the vet at the ferry dock, where she will inspect the dog and paperwork and issue the import permit. The permit is valid for three months. Continue somewhere else to check yourself and the boat in. *Fee:* Free from Monday to Friday before 4 p.m. *Experience:* After trying to figure all this out for months and skipping the area twice, we were persistent and managed to visit SVG with our dog, which is possible but hard. We had everything in order to arrive from Martinique, only to learn (after tons of unanswered email inquiries and one final phone call that got through) that this was impossible. The Government Health Certificate has to be issued in a rabies-free country, which basically only leaves St. Lucia as "previously visited country." Dogs coming from Grenada with all the required documents have been denied. Once we got in touch with the department and got the procedure straight, all went smoothly from the moment we met the vet on shore. Dr. Glasgow is very understanding, efficient, and professional to work with. *Remarks:* The information available about importing a dog in SVG states that the dog first has to fly to the U.K., await quarantine, and then be transported to SVG by plane (is there even an international airport?). The government of SVG has recently become more lenient with their rules because of cruisers wanting to visit with their dogs. You will be questioned (and told to "put your dog back on the yacht") by officials and locals in bigger towns where you walk your pet. It is recommended that you always carry your import permit with you. Even though the actual import permit and inspection are free, the costs of checking everybody into a rabies-free country prior to arriving in SVG (not a problem if you planned on visiting this island anyway), obtaining an Export Health Certificate, and making the necessary phone calls to St. Vincent to make the whole process work can add up.

GRENADA

Procedure: Ask for import permit by email/phone and get this faxed/emailed to you. *Fee:* Free
Experience: When checking into Grenada, pets have to be declared on the customs form, but no questions are asked. It is recommended that you have the dog's paperwork on board and that you act responsibly. *Remarks:* No response is given when using the government email address. Use the personal email address instead. Calling works best.

TRINIDAD AND TOBAGO

Procedure: Every pet to officially be landed in Trinidad requires a 1-6 month quarantine, unless coming from a rabies-free country where he/she resided for at least six months. *Fee:* US$ 3 (TT$ 20) per day for a 30-day quarantine, US$ 1.5 (TT$ 10) per day for a six-month quarantine, US$ 1.5 (TT$ 10) for the landing fee. *Remarks:* When checking into the country, your dog has to be declared and paperwork presented. Then he/she has to stay on the boat, which counts as quarantine.

DOMINICAN REPUBLIC

You'll need to get a health certificate issued and signed by a licensed vet. The certificate needs to contain the name and address of the owner, and complete identification of the animal (name, breed, sex, and age). Make sure it is certified by the Agriculture Department of your state and apostilled (notarized) by the state government. Have your pet examined at least 30 days prior to departure and found to be free of any infectious diseases, and have the pet treated for external and internal parasites. Your pet also needs to be vaccinated against rabies. (The rabies vaccination certificate should include the date of vaccination, established period of immunity, product name, and serial number.)

APPENDIX 3 – MUST-HAVE ITEMS FOR SAILING WITH DOGS

HOW TO SAIL WITH DOGS SURVIVAL KIT – SECURITY

COLLAR WITH ID TAGS

This is kind of a no-brainer, but it's still worth mentioning. Just about any collar will work, but we like using our homeland flags since we are an international family! For the engraved tags, we recommend getting more than one just in case they get lost. Our beagles love to run and play and wrestle and explore. Cap'n Jack has lost his tag twice, and Scout has lost hers three times. We haven't lost the actual dogs yet, but we use "SV Seefalke" rather than our actual physical home address. This way, if the dogs lose their way anywhere near the marina, their "home" can easily be found. Of course, we use both our phone numbers and include the international code (+1 for USA and +49 for Germany). Don't assume the person who finds your lost pet will know your country code.

MICROCHIP TAG

When you obtain your official microchip, you will get a tag for your dog's collar. Be sure to keep this handy if you don't want to keep it on your dog's collar. We sometimes attach these to Cap'n Jack and Scout's collars, but we generally keep them safely stored in Michelle's wallet so they're always handy. However, we keep the paperwork that comes with them in our binder with other ship documents and dog paperwork.

STRONG LEASH

We have several leashes we use. We love the Dog Whisperer leads for general walking. When the dogs have on their harnesses, we prefer leather leashes with a stainless-steel clip. At times, we also use retractable leashes so the dogs can run and play a bit without being completely unleashed.

HOW TO SAIL WITH DOGS SURVIVAL KIT – SAFETY AT SEA

MAN-OVERBOARD INDICATOR (MOBI) FOR DOGS

We use a MOBi man-overboard indicator from NASA Marine. It's a fail-safe transponder system that consists of a base unit and up to eight active transponders for crew. As soon as the base unit detects a drop in signal level, it sounds a high-intensity alarm to get everybody on board aware of the situation. The transponders are named, so a quick glance on the base unit shows who has gone overboard. On *Seefalke*, all two- and four-legged crew are wearing the MOBi transponder.

SEA FENCE

We believe strongly in having a proper sea fence to protect both the four-legged and the two-legged crew members. These are easy to install and not very expensive. The peace of mind you will have while at sea makes the time and expense completely worth it.

LIFE VEST

Human sailors aren't the only ones on board who need a proper PFD (personal flotation device). Our dogs wear one that attaches securely under the belly and around the neck. We can't stress enough how important it is to have the two handles on top of the vest. Before you set sail, find a way to let your dogs practice swimming in their live vests. They will be uncomfortable at first, but it's also important for them to have an experience swimming in them when there is not a stressful situation.

HARNESS

When we are at sea, we prefer to keep the dogs in a protective harness rather than wearing their regular collars, or in addition to their regular collars. A harness used with a strong tether is a safe way to keep them on board if a huge wave hits unexpectedly or serious conditions cause excessive heeling. The harness wraps around the dog's body rather than the neck, preventing choking or strangling if your dog slips overboard.

TETHER

We use protective tethers that are reflective and strong enough to support weights up to 90 pounds (Cap'n Jack weighs 35 pounds and Scout weighs 25 pounds). The tethers we have are 25 feet long, which gives the dogs room to roam on the boat, but the tethers can easily be shortened if the dogs' movement and access need to be restricted. These are perfect for keeping them in one spot on the deck or safely secured in the bow.

NOTE: When conditions are particularly rough, we feel more comfortable keeping Cap'n Jack and Scout secure in the main cabin and don't allow them at all on the main deck or cockpit. We have a center cockpit that is four feet deep on all sides, so this is a better option than the deck in most cases. However, in general, if we feel it's not safe, they stay below in the main cabin.

POTTY MAT

You can try to build a dog yard like Maik's, but like ours, it may face heavy sea conditions. Ours got a proper burial somewhere in The Baltic Sea. We recommend a soft fake-grass mat that has the look and feel as close to real grass as you can get. But whatever kind of mat you use, it's important to establish one place on board that your dog knows is his "spot." The secret is repetition and reward!

DOG TREATS

Our beagles love just about anything that can be called a treat! Just be sure to have plenty on hand, especially for the long sailing journeys. If you run out, try a small cracker with a little dab of peanut butter!

POO BAGS

It's important to clean up after your pet. This is simply the courteous thing to do, especially when you are a visitor in a new country. Keep plenty on board! These are also handy to have while at sea. Throw the poo overboard, but please do not throw the bags overboard!

HOW TO SAIL WITH DOGS SURVIVAL KIT – TRAVELING BY AIR

AIRLINE-APPROVED CRATES

These must be IPATA-approved for airline travel and they MUST be the correct size for your dog. We used crates by PetMate. They proved to be sturdy and airline tested. The 360-degree ventilation keeps pets comfortable with better visibility and air flow.

Cap'n Jack and Scout had to travel in separate crates, but the airline put them next to each other so they could see, hear, and smell each other.

WATER BOWLS WITH HANDLES

Especially for long flights, be sure to buy extra bowls for fresh water for your dog's flight. The small water bowls that come with the crates are not big enough. This is important! Your dog will need good hydration for the flight. We really loved these water bowls because we also can hang them out of the way on board the boat. They rarely spill thanks to the secure handles. We highly recommend these. We are still using the same water bowls that Cap'n Jack and Scout traveled with on the airplane from the U.S. to Germany.

HOW TO SAIL WITH DOGS SURVIVAL KIT – KEEPING COOL

HIGH-TECH COOLING PADS

We have never used these, but we know other sailors who travel with dogs who love them! This cooling pad keeps your pet cool and comfy with pressure-activated gel technology that absorbs body heat and delivers relief for pets from heat or joint pain. This cooling pad features a lightweight, portable, and puncture-resistant material that requires no electricity; there's no need to freeze or chill it to maintain a cool surface.

EVAPORATIVE COOLING VESTS

This is another item recommended to us by other sailors, although we have never tried it. This dog cooler comes with a three-layer cooling fabric. Soak it in cold water, wring it out, and put the cooling vest on your dog. It operates on an evaporative cooling principle. During the phase transition from liquid water to water vapor, three things happen: the temperature drops, the mesh material helps wick water, and the middle, absorbent cotton that holds the water isolates heat from the dog's skin.

FURMINATOR

This device was also recommended to us by other sailors to help remove pets' excess hair. For large dogs with long hair, the Furminator removes loose hair. It reaches through the topcoat to remove loose undercoat hair without cutting skin or damaging the topcoat (when used as directed).

WATER BOWLS

Obviously, plenty of fresh water is critical to keep your dog healthy while on land or at sea. There are some large bottles that automatically dispense water, but we don't like these. We often sail in extreme heat, making it important for us to consistently provide new, fresh, cool water for our dogs. We love the bowls that have handles or the ones that are weighted on the bottom to prevent accidental spills at sea.

WATER BOY

This is another item that we don't use, but we want to include it since we know other sailors who love it. Giving your pet water to drink in a moving vehicle or boat is a dodgy proposition—most bowls are tippy, shallow and the water winds up on the floorboards or seats more often than in your dog's mouth. This device holds up to three quarts of water in its reservoir, and it can be placed flat for easy pet access on the go. Other sailors like this, but we don't like the idea of our dogs always drinking from a plastic container.

BUDDY BOWL

Here is another item recommended by other sailors, although we can't personally recommend it. This is another option if you want a water bowl that is not as likely to spill.

HOW TO SAIL WITH DOGS SURVIVAL KIT – A FEW MORE COOL IDEAS

SEASICK SLING

We don't use one of these, but we've seen them and think they are cool! Especially if you have a small dog or one who gets seasick, place them in one of these slings to limit the motion for them and keep them feeling secure.

TOYS

Be sure to have balls, chew toys, and bones onboard to keep your dogs active and healthy. Exercise options on board are limited. We are lucky that our dogs play, wrestle, and chase each other, which gives them some exercise when we are at sea and can't take them on walks or unleash them at parks or beaches. Our dogs mostly sleep at sea.

Since they don't get as much exercise, we also don't feed them as much as we do when we are on land. But having toys available will give them some exercise.

PUZZLE BOWLS

Our beagles eat really fast. We love these puzzle bowls that not only make them work for their food, give them a little exercise, and give them a challenge, but they also help with digestion since the dogs can't devour their food quite so quickly.

BOAT LADDER AND RAMP

Another product recommended by some of our sailing friends, the Doggy Boat Ladder is an excellent choice for use with arthritic, older, or overweight pets. Your pet will find it easy to get out of the water and back aboard your vessel. This unique dog boat ramp can be attached and removed in seconds and includes a universal grip that fits almost all boat ladders with three or more steps.

APPENDIX 4 – BONUS ARTICLES & RESEARCH

I have experience sailing with dogs, but I'm not the foremost expert on the topic. As mentioned earlier, every dog is different, and every human is different. That means that each experience may be different. While doing the research, and throughout the worldwide journey, I have collected many useful tips from reading and researching. I am happy to share some of the articles and resources that have helped us along the way!

DOGS ON BOATS 101 (Shearlock, 2018)
https://theboatgalley.com/dogs-on-boats-101/

CRUISING WITH A DOG (Smitty, 2013)
https://svsmitty.wordpress.com/2013/02/08/sailingcruising-with-a-dog/

HOW TO GO LONG-DISTANCE CRUISING WITH YOUR DOG OR CAT (Bunting, 2015) http://www.yachtingworld.com/features/pets-on-board-how-to-go-long-distance-cruising-with-your-dog-or-cat-68437

4 TIPS ON SAILING WITH A DOG (Lischchynski, 2012)
http://montecristotravels.com/blog/are-you-sailing-with-a-canine-here-are-the-top-4-things-to-remember/

SAILING YOUR SALTY DOG (Wilson)
https://moderndogmagazine.com/articles/sailing-your-salty-dog/42320

FIVE TIPS FOR SAILING WITH A DOG (Sonja, 2018)
http://www.sailingncruising.com/pets/5-tips-for-sailing-with-a-dog/

SEA WEASEL – SAILING WITH DOGS (Tyler, 2009)
https://seaweasel.blogspot.com/2009/09/sailing-with-dogs.html

SAILING WITH PETS – EVERYTHING YOU NEED TO KNOW (Lilly, 2016)https://www.zizoo.com/en/magazine/sailing-pets-everything-need-know/
HOW TO TRAIN A BOAT DOG FOR SAILING (Hanes, 2017)
https://www.thewaywardhome.com/how-to-train-a-boat-dog-for-sailing/

ABOUT THE AUTHOR

MICHELLE SEGREST

Michelle Segrest has been a professional journalist for more than 30 years. She is the president of Navigate Content, Inc., a full-service content creation firm, and works hard for her clients even while sailing around the world. Michelle is a proud Southern girl from Sweet Home Alabama. She sailed for the first time with a longtime friend in Hamburg, Germany in 2013 and was immediately hooked. Sailing became a part of her soul as this journalist found a passion that would burn deeply within her forever. She still delights in researching and learning the finer details of sailing. READ MICHELLE'S LOGBOOK TO LEARN HOW TO GET YOUR SEA LEGS! WWW.NAVIGATECONTENT.COM/SAILING-ADVENTURE-BLOG

A graduate of Auburn University, Michelle has spent 30 years reporting about everything from sports to courts, lifestyles to business, politics to pastries, and technical to travel. She creates three critically-acclaimed blogs on **www.navigatecontent.com.**

Reporting on the Industry includes insightful and informative content she creates and markets for her clients in a variety of industry sectors. She covers manufacturing processes in-depth, showcases detailed problem-solving case studies, and tells the personal and professional stories of the people who are game changers in their fields. She is the author of three books on **Modern Manufacturing.**

Travel Adventures from My Office Today. Michelle firmly believes in living life by a compass and not a clock. Her home office is on Plash Island in Gulf Shores, Alabama, USA, but you won't find her there very often. She travels wherever there is an interesting story to be told, which could be anywhere on the planet. This blog covers the cool places she has explored while tracking down compelling stories for her clients.

How to Get Your Sea Legs is Michelle's award-winning blog that chronicles her adventures sailing the world for a year on a 43-foot sailboat—a journey that included an Atlantic Ocean crossing, epic battles with seasickness, remarkable wildlife encounters, and amazing destinations explored along the way. The blog made Feedspot's list of the best sailing blogs of 2019, 2020, 2021 and 2022.

Read Michelle's 3-book memoir, LIVING LIFE SIDEWAYS, available exclusively on Amazon.

REFERENCES

(n.d.). Retrieved from Sea Paws Dog Resort: www.seapawsdogresort.com

Agriculture, B. D. (n.d.). *Bahamas Import Requirements.* Retrieved from http://www.bahamas.com/sites/default/files/pdfs/bahamas_application_to_import_domestic_animals_in_tiotb.pdf

Becker, M. (2012, May 18). *How Can We Help our Seasick Dog?* Retrieved from Vet Street: http://www.vetstreet.com/dr-marty-becker/how-can-we-help-our-seasick-dog

Bring Fido. (n.d.). Retrieved from Bring Fido: www.bringfido.com

Bring Fido. (n.d.). *Airline Policies.* Retrieved from Bring Fido: www.bringfido.com/travel/airline_policies/

Bring Fido. (n.d.). *International Pet Travel.* Retrieved from Bring Fido: www.bringfido.com/travel/international/

Bring Fido. (n.d.). *Ten Tip for Flying with Fido.* Retrieved from Bring Fido: www.bringfido.com/travel/top_10_tips/

Bring Fido. (n.d.). *U.S. Pet Air Travel Regulations.* Retrieved from Bring Fido: www.bringfido.com/travel/us_regulations/

Britican, S. (2017, July 15). *Pets on Board - Sailing with a Dog on Board.* Retrieved from Sailing Britican: https://sailingbritican.com/sailing-with-a-dog/

Bunting, E. (2015, November 2). *How to Go Long Distance Cruising with your Dog or Cat.* Retrieved from Yachting World: https://www.yachtingworld.com/features/pets-on-board-how-to-go-long-distance-cruising-with-your-dog-or-cat-68437

Burkert, A. (2019, January 17). *Pet Temperature Monitor Roundup - Keep Pets Safe from the Heat.* Retrieved from Go Pet Friendly: https://blog.gopetfriendly.com/pet-temperature-monitor-roundup-devices-that-keep-pets-safe-from-the-heat/

Clark, M. (n.d.). *10 Foods That Are Bad For Dogs.* Retrieved from Dog Time: https://dogtime.com/dog-health/general/5504-bad-foods-for-dogs-list

Eveleth, R. (2012, May 14). *Do Animals Get Seasick.* Retrieved from Life Science: https://www.livescience.com/33771-animals-seasick.html

Flowers, A. (2018, May 15). *Dogs and Motion Sickness.* Retrieved from Pets WebMD: https://pets.webmd.com/dogs/dogs-and-motion-sickness#1

Flowers, A. (2018, February 5). *Foods Your Dog Should Never Eat.* Retrieved from Pets WebMD: https://pets.webmd.com/dogs/ss/slideshow-foods-your-dog-should-never-eat

Government, U. (n.d.). *Bringing Your Pet, Dog, Cat, or Ferret to the UK.* Retrieved from Governement UK: https://www.gov.uk/take-pet-abroad/print

Granshaw, L. (2013, June 3). *Boating With Dogs - 9 Safety Tips.* Retrieved from Vet Street: http://www.vetstreet.com/our-pet-experts/boating-with-dogs-9-safety-tips

Hanes, K. (2017, November 18). *How to Train a Boat Dog for Sailing.* Retrieved from The Wayward Home: https://www.thewaywardhome.com/how-to-train-a-boat-dog-for-sailing/

IPATA. (n.d.). Retrieved from International Pet and Animal Transportation Association: https:/www.ipata.org

Langsdon, A. (2018, September 22). *Dog Approved People Food.* Retrieved from Cesar's Way : https://www.cesarsway.com/dog-approved-people-food/

Lee, H. (1960). *To Kill A Mockingbird.* New York: J.B. Lippincott & Co.

Liesbet, S. I. (n.d.). *Cruising the Eastern Caribbean with Your Dog.* Retrieved from Coastal Boating: http://cruising.coastalboating.net/Destinations/Carib/CruisingECwithDog.html

Lilly. (2016, February 17). *Sailing with Pets - Everything You Need to Know.* Retrieved from Zizoo: https://www.zizoo.com/en/magazine/sailing-pets-everything-need-know/

Lischchynski, S. (2012, January 21). *4 Tips on Sailing with a Dog.* Retrieved from Monte Cristo Travel: http://montecristotravels.com/blog/are-you-sailing-with-a-canine-here-are-the-top-4-things-to-remember/

Lufthansa. (n.d.). Retrieved from Lufthansa: www.lufthansa.com

Miller, D. B. (2017, November 12). *20 Tips on How to Keep Dogs Warm in the Winter.* Retrieved from Top Dog Tips: https://topdogtips.com/how-to-keep-dogs-warm-in-the-winter/

Moss, L. (2014, October 8). *12 Human Foods Dogs Can Eat and 5 They Shouldn't.* Retrieved from Mother Nature Network: https://www.mnn.com/family/pets/stories/11-human-foods-dogs-can-eat-and-5-they-shouldnt

Noon Site. (n.d.). Retrieved from Noon Site: www.noonsite.com

Pamela. (n.d.). *The Most Surprising Ways to Keep Your Dog Cool on the Boat.* Retrieved from Something Wagging This Way Comes: https://www.somethingwagging.com/the-most-surprising-ways-to-keep-your-dog-cool-on-the-boat/

Pet Air Carrier. (n.d.). Retrieved from Pet Air Carrier: www.petaircarrier.com

Pet Travel. (n.d.). Retrieved from Pet Travel: www.pettravel.com

Schenker, M. (2018, August 24). *What Foods are Toxic for Dogs?* Retrieved from Canine Journal: https://www.caninejournal.com/foods-not-to-feed-dog/

Segrest, M. (2018, August 27). *Helgoland, Obstacles, The North Sea & Puppy Cranes.* Retrieved from Sailors & Seadogs: https://www.sailorsandseadogs.com/blog-old/helgoland-north-sea?rq=Puppy%20cranes

Segrest, M. (2018, August 24). *The Baltic Sea - She's a Mean Girl.* Retrieved from Sailors & Seadogs: https://www.sailorsandseadogs.com/blog-old/sailing-baltic-sea

Segrest, M. (2018, November 15). *Walking the Armadillos.* Retrieved from Sailors & Seadogs: https://www.sailorsandseadogs.com/blog-old/rabat-casablanca-tangier-morocco-africa

Shojai, A. (2019, May 6). *Heat Stroke Symptoms in Puppies.* Retrieved from The Spruce Pets: https://www.thesprucepets.com/puppy-heat-stroke-2804958

Smitty, J. K. (2013, February 8). *Sailing/Cruising with a Dog.* Retrieved from SV Smitty: https://svsmitty.wordpress.com/2013/02/08/sailingcruising-with-a-dog/

Sonja. (2018, January 4). *Five Tips for Sailing with a Dog.* Retrieved from Sailing n Cruising: http://www.sailingncruising.com/pets/5-tips-for-sailing-with-a-dog/

Shearlock, C. (2016, January 11). *Getting a Bahamas Pet Permit.* Retrieved from The Boat Galley: https://theboatgalley.com/getting-a-bahamas-pet-permit/

Shearlock, C. (2018, December 28). *Dogs on Boats 101.* Retrieved from The Boat Galley: https://theboatgalley.com/dogs-on-boats-101/

Staff, A. (2019, January 3). *Human Foods Dogs Can and Can't Eat.* Retrieved from AKC: https://www.akc.org/expert-advice/nutrition/human-foods-dogs-can-and-cant-eat/

Stregowski, J. (2019, March 30). *How to Identify Heat Stroke Symptoms in Dogs.* Retrieved from The Spruce Pets: https://www.thesprucepets.com/heat-stroke-in-dogs-1117860

Stregowski, J. (2019, March 29). *How to Keep Your Dogs Cool in the Heat.* Retrieved from The Spruce Pets: https://www.thesprucepets.com/keeping-dogs-cool-in-the-heat-1117451

Trekkers, L. H. (2019). *How to Get an EU Pet Passport.* Retrieved from Long Haul Trekkers: https://longhaultrekkers.com/how-to-get-an-eu-pet-passport/

Tyler. (2009, September 3). *Sailing with Dogs.* Retrieved from Sea Weasel: https://seaweasel.blogspot.com/2009/09/sailing-with-dogs.html

USDA. (2018, July 30). *United States Department of Agriculture.* Retrieved from APHIS - USDA: www.aphis.usda.gov/aphis/pet-travel-european_union_pet_passports

Wilson, G. (n.d.). *Sailing Your Salty Dog.* Retrieved from Modern Dog Magazine: https://moderndogmagazine.com/articles/sailing-your-salty-dog/42320

100 TIPS

*Here is a recap of **100 Tips for a Pet-Friendly Voyage!***

PET-FRIENDLY BOATS

1. Be sure you have a sturdy sea rail.
2. Add a sea fence net to prevent accidental overboard incidents.
3. Clear the deck of lines and other obstacles.
4. Make the companionways pet-friendly by making them less steep and by removing obstacles.
5. Protect anything that can be destroyed by chewing.
6. Provide the dogs with some space of their own.
7. Consider sailing with a self-draining cockpit and deck, which are helpful for accidents.
8. Any areas that you can't make pet-friendly, block off and declare them no-pet zones.
9. If the design of your boat is not suitable for pet safety and you can't outfit it to be safe, don't sail with your dogs on that boat.

TRAVEL WITH DOGS BY AIR

10. Research and plan early—at least two months before flight.
11. Locate an IPATA-approved pet carrier if flying from or to the U.S.
12. Order the necessary crates and supplies early.
13. Help your dog adapt to the crate well in advance of the flight.
14. Work closely with your veterinarian to get all shots and necessary paperwork taken care of early.
15. Create and invest in a first-aid kit for your pet.
16. Carefully research the regulations of your departure and arrival countries.
17. Be prepared for long customs procedures at the sites of departure and arrival.
18. Book a direct flight, if possible.
19. Avoid giving your dog a sedative for the flight. Our veterinarian strongly urged us to resist this temptation as it could cause other medical issues for your pet.
20. Visit a local veterinarian at the arrival country to secure a European Pet Passport and other required documents.
21. Have plenty of water and extra food available for the flight.
22. Pack your pet's favorite blanket and toys in the travel crate.

23. Give your dog a chance to run and play unleashed upon arrival.

TRAVEL WITH DOGS BY SEA

24. Research every country you may want to visit for entry and customs requirements.
25. Use online resources like Noon Site, Bring Fido, and Travel Pet to learn about general requirements.
26. Visit the website of each country for specific and updated requirements.
27. Research surrounding countries of your destination, just in case weather or other factors cause you to change plans.
28. Avoid countries that require quarantine.

FIRST AID FOR DOGS AT SEA

29. Consult with your veterinarian before sailing with pets.
30. Secure all required shots and paperwork.
31. Ask your veterinarian to help you create a first-aid kit for your pet.
32. Be aware of any allergies your pet may have.
33. In addition to first-aid supplies, be sure to bring enough of your pet's regular medications or supplies.
34. First-aid kit should contain preventive medicines as well as emergency medicine and supplies.
35. Ask your veterinarian if you can text him/her while at sea in case of emergency.
36. Familiarize yourself with the uses for each medication on board.
37. Keep medications in a place that's easy to access when underway.
38. Make sure all medicine is labeled correctly.
39. Research local veterinarians near each port you may visit, just in case of emergency.
40. Create a "cheat sheet" to help you quickly identify appropriate medications for different scenarios.
41. Learn how to apply bandages and practice before you set sail.
42. Know the signs of seasickness in animals.

SAFETY AT SEA

43. Apply similar safety procedures for your four-legged crew as you do for your two-legged crew.
44. Take all precautions to avoid man- or pet-overboard situations.
45. Install a sea fence net.

46. Establish good-weather and bad-weather potty routines.
47. Have backup plans for bad or unsafe weather.
48. If you are unsure that conditions are safe for your pet, keep them in a secure cabin below deck.
49. Install life lines and tethering lines.
50. Use light-reflective gear.
51. Equip your pet with secure life vests.
52. Keep retrieval nets and hooks easily available to help retrieve pets if they go overboard.
53. Equip your pet with Man Overboard Transponders (MOBi).
54. Establish and practice Man Overboard procedures.

POTTY TRAINING

55. Establish a safe place on board that will be your pet's "place to go."
56. Purchase a fake-grass mat, or build a dog yard with real grass, and leave it in the designated spot.
57. If needed, place a pee or poo sample on the mat so your dog will recognize the scent.
58. Put your dogs on a leash and "walk" them to their place, as if you were taking them on a walk.
59. Use treats, praise and rewards, and do this consistently.
60. Keep a spare mat on board to use in a different spot when conditions are unsafe to go to the regular designated spot.
61. Establish a potty routine (this may be different on land, at sea, and at anchorage).
62. When it doesn't rain for a while, clean the deck around the potty area more often.

FEEDING SAILING DOGS

63. Research human foods that are ok for your dogs, and those that are dangerous.
64. If your dog requires special dog food, don't count on it being available in every country you visit. Provision accordingly.
65. Keep your veterinarian's phone number handy.
66. Keep the phone number for poison control handy.
67. Establish "at sea" and "in port" eating routines.

ESTABLISH A ROUTINE

68. Establish routines for your pet, based on whether you are at sea, at anchorage, on the hard, or in port.
69. Routines should include how and where they sleep, how and when they exercise, and how much food to feed them.
70. Adjust your pet's calorie intake based on how much exercise he/she is getting.
71. Most animals don't have a concept of time, but they tend to understand the order of things. Establish a routine that includes a specific order of doing things.
72. Whatever routines you establish for your pets, always be consistent.

WHEN IT'S NOT DOG FRIENDLY

73. Study the culture before visiting a new country to learn about its attitude toward pets.
74. Be respectful of the local culture.
75. Be sure your dogs are "fixed" (spayed or neutered) just in case they run into stray animals that are most likely not fixed.
76. If you are unsure of the culture's attitude toward animals, keep your dog on a leash at all times.
77. In addition to the required shots, be sure your dog is up to date on other shots that could be helpful in foreign lands where other diseases and parasites may be evident.

STAYING WARM

78. Keep your dogs out of the cold wind, preferably in the cabin where there is some insulation.
79. Use sleeping bags or even a doggie sweater to help your dogs stay warm.
80. Don't let your dogs sleep outside. Keep them inside where there is some protection from harsh wind and weather.
81. Keep your dog dry. If he gets splashed by a wave, dry him quickly to prevent extra chill.
82. Feed your dog extra calories to fuel his internal thermostat.
83. Don't go swimming.
84. Cuddle up. Our dogs love to cuddle with us and with each other. Human body warmth is a great way to keep your dog warm.

KEEPING COOL

85. Always have fresh, cool water for your pet to drink.
86. Cover your deck with a tarp or sail. Make sure there is shade for your dog.

87. If it's safe, let your dog take a swim in the cool ocean. If your dog doesn't like to get in the water (like Cap'n Jack and Scout), then use a bucket or hose to douse them with cool water as often as possible to cool them off.
88. If you have a long-haired dog, keep him well groomed to minimize his natural fur coat.
89. If you have a fan and access to electricity, keep it blowing to circulate the air in the cabin.
90. While sailing, if the conditions are safe, let your dog come out onto the deck or into the cockpit so he can enjoy the cool breeze.
91. Consider using cooling dog beds or cooling pads. We haven't tried these, but we know sailors who use them.
92. If you have a fridge or freezer onboard, try wetting a towel or bandana and leaving it in the fridge for a while, then wrap the cool, wet cloth around their neck.
93. Avoid long walks in the extreme heat.
94. Be aware of the signs of overheating and react quickly to them.

LONG-DISTANCE CRUISING

95. Be patient. The dog will learn to do its business on board, even if it takes a few days. No worries.
96. Stock up on food when you have the chance.
97. Have some games for the dog so that it doesn't get bored on the boat.
98. Bring with you any pet-required internet research.
99. In the Caribbean:
    a. In Saint Lucia many locals are afraid of dogs or don't like dogs.
    b. On the other hand, dogs seem to be very welcome in French islands such as Martinique, Guadeloupe, etc. People here seem to like dogs and it is no problem to take a dog to a restaurant.
    c. Any non-French island: never bring a dog to a restaurant.
    d. Avoid beaches with people as a courtesy.
    e. Do not take a dog to National Park beaches, such as St. Thomas or the U.S. Virgin Islands.
100. So far, no vet has checked the microchip. We wouldn't recommend going without it, though.

Printed in Great Britain
by Amazon